# Peterson
# First Guide
## to
# ASTRONOMY

### Jay M. Pasachoff

Star maps by
**Wil Tirion**

Constellation paintings by
**Robin Brickman**

HOUGHTON
MIFFLIN
COMPANY
•
BOSTON
NEW YORK

Some information updated 1997.

For information about this and other Houghton Mifflin
trade and reference books and multimedia products, visit
The Bookstore at Houghton Mifflin on the World Wide Web at
http://www.hmco.com/trade/.

PETERSON FIRST GUIDES,
PETERSON FIELD GUIDES, and
PETERSON FIELD GUIDE SERIES
are registered trademarks of
Houghton Mifflin Company.

Library of Congress Cataloging-in-Publication Data

Pasachoff, Jay M.
Peterson first guide to Astronomy.
Cover title: Peterson first guides. Astronomy.
Includes index.
Summary: A basic field guide for beginning observers
of the night sky, introducing information on the loca-
tions, and other bodies in outer space.
1. Astronomy—Juvenile literature.  2. Stars—
Atlases—Juvenile literature.  3. Astronomy—
Amateurs' manuals.  [1. Astronomy—Observers'
manuals.  2. Stars.  3. Constellations]
I. Peterson, Roger Tory, date.  II. Tirion, Wil, ill.
III. Brickman, Robin, ill.  IV. Title.
QB46.P376  1986  522  87-26143
**ISBN  0-395-93542-3**

Printed in Italy

NIL  18  17  16  15

# Editor's Note

In 1934, my *Field Guide to the Birds* first saw the light of day. The book was designed so that live birds could be readily identified at a distance without resorting to the technical points specialists use. The Peterson Field Guide Series, which has now grown to over 30 volumes on a wide range of subjects, has enabled millions of users to learn about plants, animals, rocks, and stars without specialized training. It is a special pleasure to present a guide to the stars, which everybody can see. Anyone interested in birds or other aspects of nature should surely be interested in the stars.

Even though Peterson Field Guides are intended for the novice as well as the expert, there are still many beginners who would like something simpler to start with—a smaller guide that would give them confidence. It is for this audience—those who perhaps recognize the moon and maybe the Big Dipper but little else—that the First Guides have been created. They offer a selection of things that you would want to see when you are beginning. Since the sky is accessible to everyone, it is fitting that this *First Guide to Astronomy* should be one of the earliest in this series. This First Guide, like others in the series, makes it easy to get started in the field. We hope that you will enjoy it and learn from it, and that you may one day want to graduate to the full-fledged Peterson *Field Guide to the Stars and Planets.*

Roger Tory Peterson

# Introducing Astronomy

The sun and moon, the stars and planets, and the other objects in the sky are always with us. Wherever we live, wherever we travel, we can always call upon the companionship of these familiar things. No equipment is necessary to see them, but a knowledge of what you are looking at will add to your appreciation and enjoyment.

Have you ever tried counting the stars in the sky? In a dark place on a clear night, with your unaided eyes, you can see about 3000 stars. From a city street, with street lights polluting the sky with their brightness, you may see only a handful. As the Earth turns, the stars appear to move across the sky. The speed at which they appear to move depends on where they are in the sky. The fastest of them appear to move, every hour, across an arc of sky covered by the width of your fist at the end of your outstretched arm. Over a few hours, the appearance of the sky changes drastically. And from season to season, as autumn changes into winter or spring into summer, different stars become visible in the evening.

To show what is in the sky as it changes through the night or through the year, this book contains 24 star maps (see pp. 20–43). Each month of the year has its own pair, one map to be used when you face north and the other, when you face south. The maps are meant for observers at midnorthern latitudes.

The maps show stick figures for the constellations, the arrangements of stars described long ago and often associated with myths and legends. The pages following the maps show some of the most popular and easy-to-see constellations in more detail. For other topics, see:

This book is meant for naked-eye observing. If you have binoculars, some fainter objects will become visible, a few of which are listed here. If you have a telescope, you can look at a few of the objects in this book in more detail. At the end of the book I answer common questions about using binoculars or telescopes.

How to start using this book? I would suggest that you begin by reading the first 19 pages. Then, on the next clear night, find the star maps (pp. 20–43) that match the date and time. Match the constellations on the map with the stars in the sky. Read about a few of those constellations in more detail (pp. 44–67), and carry on from there.

Enjoy the sky! Enjoy astronomy!

The W of stars in the sky is the constellation Cassiopeia; it is seen here over Zion National Park.

# Observing the Stars

Each night, many stars appear to rise above the horizon, travel across part of the sky, and eventually sink below the horizon. Others remain visible all night long. If you face east, you will see stars rise in the night sky. They won't be moving fast enough for you to see their motion, but if you look back at the sky after a while, you will see they are in different places.

One-third to halfway up the sky in the north is a point around which the stars appear to rotate. This imaginary point, the *celestial north pole,* appears never to move in the sky. It lies directly above the Earth's north pole. Halfway between the celestial north and south poles, lying over the Earth's equator, is the *celestial equator.*

If we were at the Earth's north pole, the celestial north pole would be right above our heads—at the point called our *zenith* (zee'nith). Wherever you are, the zenith is the point in the sky directly above you. As we move from the north pole toward the equator, the celestial north pole appears lower in the sky, until, at the equator, it is on the horizon. The height of the celestial north pole above the horizon corresponds to the latitude where you are observing. At the 40° North latitude of New York City, for example, the celestial north pole is 40° above the horizon.

All stars appear to move in circles around the celestial pole. Stars close to each pole move in small circles and never go below the horizon. We call them *circumpolar.*

Facing east from the latitudes of the United States, stars appear to rise at an angle from the horizon. For this photo, of Orion, the camera shutter was left open for many minutes, so the stars would trail upward; next, the camera shutter was closed and then opened for a few seconds to make the point images of the stars.

Stars farther from the pole move in circles so large that part of the circle lies below our horizon. We see those stars rising toward the eastern part of the sky and, later, setting in the western part of the sky. The circles are so big that the paths of the stars look almost straight.

The celestial south pole is an imaginary point above the Earth's south pole. Neither the celestial south pole nor the stars near it are ever visible from our latitudes. Only if we go south of the Earth's equator can we see them.

Each night, the stars rise about four minutes earlier than the night before. Thus a given star rises an hour earlier every 15 days. As a result, we see different stars in different seasons (see p. 69). This effect occurs because the Earth rotates on its axis as it revolves around the sun. As the Earth travels $\frac{1}{365}$ of the way around the sun each day, it also makes one full turn (rotation) on its axis. Thus we are facing a slightly different part of the sky at the same time each night: the stars will appear to have traveled 3 minutes 56 seconds per day farther around the sky, even though it is the Earth that is actually moving in relation to the stars. We face the same stars 3 minutes and 56 seconds (that is, 24 hours divided by 365 days) earlier each day.

Stars trail around the celestial north pole, an imaginary point above the Earth's north pole.

## Brightness and Magnitude

Thousands of years ago, the Greek astronomer Hipparchus said, reasonably, that the brightest stars were "of the first magnitude," the next brightest stars were "of the second magnitude," and so on. The faintest stars visible to the naked eye were "of the sixth magnitude." Today, we still use a version of this method of describing brightness. How bright a star appears to be is called its *apparent magnitude.*

Modern astronomers have made the magnitude scale more precise. A difference of·five magnitudes now means exactly 100 times in brightness. A star of magnitude 1.5 is between magnitude 1 and magnitude 2. Also, some objects are even brighter than the group of stars called 1st-magnitude stars. These stars can have a magnitude of zero or even negative numbers. The brightest star in the sky, Sirius, has a magnitude of $-1.5$.

Every difference of one magnitude corresponds to a factor of about 2.5 in brightness. For example, a 2nd-magnitude star is about 2.5 times fainter than a 1st-magnitude star. A 6th-magnitude star is exactly 100 times fainter than a 1st-magnitude star.

### Magnitudes of Selected Objects

| | |
|---|---|
| Venus, at its brightest | $-4$ |
| Jupiter, at its brightest | $-3$ |
| Sirius, the brightest star | $-1.5$ |
| Arcturus, a bright star | 0 |
| Pointers, at the end of the Big Dipper | 2 |
| Faintest stars on our star maps | 4.5 |
| Faintest stars visible to the naked eye | 6 |
| Faintest stars with binoculars | 9 |
| Faintest stars with small telescope | 12 |
| Faintest stars with biggest telescope | 25 |

How faint a star you can see depends on how much light passes into your eye. At night, the pupil in your eye can open as wide as 8mm. Your brain processes a new image every 1/30 second or so. You can, therefore, detect only as much light as comes into an 8-mm circle in 1/30 second.

If you use binoculars, you collect light from a larger circle—the area of each front, or objective, lens. Each front lens of 7 × 50 binoculars, a common type for use in astronomy, is 50mm in diameter. Since this lens collects more light than your naked eye can, you can see fainter objects when you use binoculars.

Telescopes generally have larger lenses (or mirrors) than binoculars have. Thus they collect even more light and allow you to see still fainter objects (see p. 120). Another way to collect more light is to collect it for a longer time by using a camera. Whereas the eye collects light for only $\frac{1}{30}$ of a second per image, film can be exposed for many seconds or minutes. This, too, allows you to see fainter objects.

## The Brightest Stars in Our Sky
## (visible from midnorthern latitudes)

| Star | Constellation | Magnitude | Visible in Evening |
|------|---------------|-----------|--------------------|
| Sirius | Canis Major (Maps 1S–4S, 12S) | − 1.5 | winter |
| Arcturus | Boötes (Maps 2N, 3, 4S, 6S, 7, 8N) | 0.0 | spring |
| Vega | Lyra (Maps 4N–6N, 9N–11N) | 0.0 | summer |
| Capella | Auriga (Maps 2N–5N, 8N–11N) | + 0.1 | winter |
| Rigel | Orion (Maps 1S–3S, 11S–12S) | + 0.1 | winter |
| Procyon | Canis Minor (Maps 1S–4S, 11, 12S) | + 0.4 | spring |
| Betelgeuse | Orion (Maps 1S–4S, 10N, 11S–12S) | + 0.5 | winter |
| Altair | Aquila (Maps 5N, 6S–10S, 11) | + 0.8 | summer |
| Aldebaran | Taurus (Maps 1S–3S, 10, 11S–12S) | + 0.9 | winter |
| Antares | Scorpius (Maps 5S–8S) | + 1.0 | summer |
| Spica | Virgo (Maps 3S–7S) | + 1.0 | summer |
| Pollux | Gemini (Maps 1S, 12S) | + 1.1 | spring |

* The maps showing bright stars and constellations appear on pp. 20–43. N = facing north; S = facing south. On some dates and times, the stars are higher in the sky than the regions shown on the maps.

# Estimating Distances Across the Sky

To find your way from one star or constellation to the next, it is often convenient to be able to estimate angles in the sky. The distance (measured in degrees of arc) from the horizon in any direction to the zenith, the point overhead, is 90°. Your fist, held at the end of your outstretched arm, takes up about 10°. Your thumb, held at the end of your outstretched arm, takes up about 2°. The moon covers about ½°.

From our midnorthern latitudes, the Big Dipper can be seen at all times of year. It is an *asterism*, a group of stars making up a special shape, rather than a *constellation*, one of the 88 regions into which the sky is divided (see p. 12). The stars at the end of the bowl, which is at the right in the photograph below, are called the Pointers, because a line drawn through them curves across the sky almost directly to Polaris, the North Star. The Pointers are separated by about 5°, and the angle, or apparent distance, from the top star in the Pointers to the North Star is about 30°. You can judge 30° either by taking one-third the distance from the horizon to the zenith or by taking three fists' width across the sky.

The Big Dipper.

The constellation Orion (p. 46) is perhaps the easiest to find in the sky when it is "up," that is, when it is above the horizon, as it is on winter evenings. Three 2nd-magnitude stars make up its "belt," which is 3° long.

Two bright stars appear symmetrically above and below Orion's belt, each about 9° (almost one fist's width) away. Betelgeuse, in Orion's shoulder, is slightly reddish even to the naked eye. We thus know it is a cool star. Rigel, in Orion's heel, glows noticeably blue-white, indicating that it is a hot star.

In the midst of Orion's sword, which extends downward from the left side of his belt, a fuzzy region glows. This is a region of gas and dust, called the Orion Nebula, in which stars are forming. It is not visible to the naked eye, but appears faintly in binoculars or telescopes.

The constellation Orion, with reddish Betelgeuse at top left, blue-white Rigel at bottom right, the belt in the center, and the sword with the Orion Nebula extending downward. The reddish color shows only on long exposures.

11

# The Constellations

People have long pretended that the sky is divided into groups of stars, each group with its own story. Each civilization has had its own legends. Many of the constellation names we use today come from the ancient Greeks. The northern sky is largely covered with these constellations, since that is the part of the sky that was visible from the Greek empire. When scientific expeditions went to the southern hemisphere a few hundred years ago, they charted the regions of the sky that could not be studied from our latitudes. The constellation names assigned to the southern constellations in the 17th and 18th centuries often reflect more modern ideas and a fascination with mechanical devices.

Though many constellation names have been in use for centuries, the International Astronomical Union in 1930 agreed to divide the entire sky into exactly 88 constellations. Each star now belongs to one and only one constellation. Some constellations are too far south for us to see; they are printed in *italics* in the table on pp. 13–14.

Starting on p. 44, we discuss a few constellations in detail. Many people know the 12 constellations of the *zodiac*, the ones that form a backdrop for most of the sun's path across the sky. They are shown in **boldface**. Of course, these constellations are not visible when the sun is passing through them, because it is then daytime!

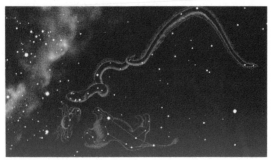

Many civilizations have stories about figures in the sky.

# The Constellations

| | |
|---|---|
| Andromeda* | an-drom'e-da |
| Antlia, the Pump | ant'lee-a |
| *Apus, the Bird of Paradise* | ah'pus |
| **Aquarius, the Water Bearer** | a-quayr'ee-us |
| Aquila, the Eagle | ak'will-a |
| *Ara, the Altar* | ah'ra |
| **Aries, the Ram** | air'ees |
| Auriga, the Charioteer | oar-eye'ja |
| Boötes, the Herdsman | bo-o'tees |
| Caelum, the Chisel | see'lum |
| Camelopardalis, the Giraffe | ka'mel-o-par-dal'is |
| **Cancer, the Crab** | kan'ser |
| Canes Venatici, the Hunting Dogs | kay'nes ve-na'ti-chi |
| Canis Major, the Big Dog | kay'nis ma'jer |
| Canis Minor, the Little Dog | kay'nis mye'ner |
| **Capricornus, the Goat** | kap'ri-korn-us |
| *Carina, the Ship's Keel* | kar-eye'na |
| Cassiopeia* | kass-ee-oh'pee-a |
| *Centaurus, the Centaur* | sen-taw'rus |
| Cepheus* | see'fee-us |
| Cetus, the Whale | see'tus |
| *Chamaeleon, the Chamaeleon* | ka-meel'yon |
| *Circinus, the Compass* | sir'sin-us |
| Columba, the Dove | kah-lum'ba |
| Coma Berenices, Berenice's Hair | koh'ma beh-reh-nee'ses |
| Corona Australis, the Southern Crown | koh-roh'na aus-tral'is |
| Corona Borealis, the Northern Crown | koh-roh'na baw-ree-al'is |
| Corvus, the Crow | koar'vus |
| Crater, the Cup | kray'ter |
| *Crux, the Southern Cross* | krucks |
| Cygnus, the Swan | sig'nus |
| Delphinus, the Dolphin | del-fee'nus |
| *Dorado, the Swordfish* | daw-rah'doh |
| Draco, the Dragon | dray'ko |
| Equuleus, the Little Horse | eh-kwoo'lee-us |
| *Eridanus** | ey-rid'an-us |
| Fornax, the Furnace | four'nax |
| **Gemini, the Twins** | gem'en-eye |
| *Grus, the Crane* | grus |
| Hercules* | her'kyool-ees |
| Horologium, the Clock | haw-roh-loj'ee-um |
| Hydra, the Water Snake | hye'dra |
| *Hydrus, the Water Snake* | hye'drus |
| *Indus, the Indian* | in'dus |
| Lacerta, the Lizard | la-sir'ta |
| **Leo, the Lion** | lee'oh |
| Leo Minor, the Little Lion | lee'oh mye'ner |
| Lepus, the Rabbit | lee'pus |
| **Libra, the Scales** | lee'bra |
| Lupus, the Wolf | loo'pus |
| Lynx, the Lynx | links |
| Lyra, the Harp | lye'ra |

| | |
|---|---|
| *Mensa, the Table* | men'sa |
| Microscopium, the Microscope | mye-kroh-scohp'ee-um |
| Monoceros, the Unicorn | mon-oh-seyr'us |
| *Musca, the Fly* | mus'ka |
| *Norma, the Surveyor's Level* | norm'a |
| *Octans, the Octant* | ok'tans |
| Ophiuchus* | oh-fee-you'kus |
| Orion* | oh-rye'un |
| *Pavo, the Peacock* | pa'voh |
| Pegasus* | peg'a-sus |
| Perseus* | per'see-us |
| *Phoenix, the Phoenix* | fee'nicks |
| *Pictor, the Easel* | pik'tor |
| **Pisces, the Fish** | pye'sees |
| Pisces Austrinus, the Southern Fish | pye'sees aws-trye'nus |
| Puppis, the Ship's Stern | pup'pis |
| Pyxis, the Ship's Compass | pick'sis |
| *Reticulum, the Net* | reh-tick'you-lum |
| Sagitta, the Arrow | sa-jet'a |
| **Sagittarius, the Archer** | sa-jet-air'ee-us |
| **Scorpius, the Scorpion** | skawr'pee-us |
| Sculptor, the Sculptor | skulp'ter |
| Scutum, the Shield | skyoo'tum |
| Serpens, the Sextant | sir'pens |
| **Taurus, the Bull** | taw'rus |
| Telescopium, the Telescope | tel-es-koh'pee-um |
| Triangulum, the Triangle | trye-ang'you-lum |
| *Triangulum Australe, the Southern Triangle* | trye-ang'you-lum aws-tray'lee |
| *Tucana, the Toucan* | too-kay'na |
| Ursa Major, the Big Bear | er'sa may'jer |
| Ursa Minor, the Little Bear | er'sa mye'ner |
| *Vela, the Ship's Sails* | vee'la |
| **Virgo, the Virgin** | vir'go |
| *Volans, the Flying Fish* | voh'lans |
| Vulpecula, the Little Fox | vul-pek'you-la |

Alternative pronunciations sometimes exist. * Proper name.
**Boldface:** zodiac; *italics:* too far south to see from 40° North latitude.

# The Milky Way

On a clear night in a dark place, when the moon is not full, you may see a hazy white band stretching across the sky. This band is the *Milky Way*. Even with the naked eye, you can see that the Milky Way is not regular; it has patches of white and darker regions.

The fact that the Milky Way is a narrow band in the sky tells us that we live in a flat galaxy (p. 78). Imagine that the Milky Way is shaped like a dinner plate. If we were tiny people living on that plate, standing about two-thirds of the way toward the edge from the center, the plate would look to us as the Milky Way does. If we looked toward the edge or toward the center, we would see lots of plate; in the sky we see lots of stars and clouds of gas and dust, which are called *nebulae* (see p. 70). But looking up from the plate, we see none of it. Looking up or down from our spot in our flat galaxy, we see only the stars nearest us.

The Milky Way is shown on the star maps on pp. 20–43. On summer evenings, it passes nearly overhead, through the constellation Cygnus, the Swan, and through the constellation Sagittarius, the Archer, in the south. When we look at Sagittarius, we are looking toward the center of our galaxy, which looks richer in stars, gas, and dust. Scanning the Milky Way with binoculars reveals many such fuzzy regions.

The Milky Way, as seen when looking in the direction of the center of our galaxy, which is in the constellation Sagittarius.

# Telling Stars from Planets

Though the stars appear to move across the sky in the course of the night, their positions in relation to each other remain fixed. But there are a few points of light in the sky that from night to night change position slightly with respect to the stars. These are the planets, from the Greek word for "wanderer." Telescopes revealed that the planets have different shapes (Mercury and Venus have phases, for example, and Saturn has a ring) and sizes. Now that we have sent spacecraft up close to most of the planets, we have learned a great deal more about their basic natures (see pp. 84–99).

You can remember the planets' names, in order of distance from the sun, by the first letters of "My Very Educated Mother Just Sent Us Nine Pizzas": Mercury Venus Earth Mars Jupiter Saturn Uranus Neptune Pluto. But how do you find them in the sky?

## Twinkling Stars and Steady Planets

The stars usually appear to twinkle in the sky. They are tiny points of light beyond Earth's atmosphere, and the shimmering and shaking of our atmosphere make their images appear to change in brightness from moment to moment and to dance around. The planets are small disks, though we cannot detect their size with our unaided eyes. The different parts of their images change and move differently, so the total image of a planet is much steadier than that of a star. When you see a celestial object shine steadily while others around it are twinkling, you are probably looking at a planet.

## The Position of the Planets

The orbit of Venus around the sun is inside that of the Earth, so Venus never appears very far from the sun in the sky. When Venus is visible, it is the brightest object in the sky other than the sun and moon. If you see a bright object shining steadily in the western sky at or after sunset, or in the eastern sky at or before sunrise, you are probably looking at Venus.

Jupiter can also be very bright. It can appear in the sky even at midnight. If you see a bright object shining steadily in the southern half of the sky, far from where the sun set or will rise, you are probably looking at Jupiter.

Mars rarely becomes as bright as Jupiter or Venus, and Saturn never becomes that bright, but they still shine steadily in the sky. Mars has a reddish tinge, which is visible even with the naked eye. Saturn appears slightly yellowish. Binoculars are needed to see Uranus or Neptune, and it takes a telescope to see Pluto.

## *The Path of the Planets*

The Earth and the other planets orbit the sun more or less in the same flat plane, that is, as though they were all lying on a dish. Thus the sun and the planets all appear to travel along the same path across the sky. This path, which is traveled precisely by the sun and approximately by the other planets, is called the *ecliptic.*

The ecliptic is shown as a dotted line on the star maps on pp. 20–43. You will always find the planets close to the ecliptic.

The positions of the planets change from week to week and do not repeat from year to year. If a planet is "up," you can find it by looking for a steady object near the ecliptic.

Through any small telescope or binoculars, you can see four moons around Jupiter. You can also see belts on the planet, though this exposure, made for the moons, is too long to show them. You can also see Saturn, with its rings, and its largest moon, in a small telescope or binoculars.

# How to Use the Star Maps

The pages that follow contain pairs of star maps, each good for certain dates and times. The first map of each pair is for use when you are facing north, and the second is for use when you are facing south. Together they show most of the sky, although the very top of the sky, the circle 30° in radius around the zenith, is not shown. The bright star Vega, for example, is near the zenith on summer evenings, though it is too high to appear on Maps 7 and 8 (facing north).

The dates and times for which each pair of maps can be used are shown along the bottom. The next pair of maps shows the sky either one month later at the same time or on the same date two hours later.

The maps show all stars brighter than magnitude 4.5 and a few fainter ones; you should be able to see all of these stars if you are in a dark place far from cities and with a clear horizon. The area closest to the horizon—the bottom 10° or more, equivalent to your fist at the end of your outstretched arm against the sky or to a thumb's width on the star map—is usually masked by haze or buildings and is therefore hard to see.

Names and colors are shown for all stars that are 1st magnitude or brighter. The colors of stars reveal their temperatures: bluish white stars (types O and B) are the hottest, yellower stars like the sun (type G) are cooler, and reddish stars (type M) are the coolest. (See key on p. 19.)

Some stars (such as Mira in the constellation Cetus) vary in brightness and are shown as open circles on the maps. *Double stars*, pairs or a few stars orbiting each other, are marked with a horizontal line through them. In some regions of space, many stars are found close together. These *star clusters* come in two kinds. *Open clusters* like the Pleiades and the Hyades (see p. 56) are made up of many young stars formed close to each other. *Globular clusters*, marked with dotted circles, are many old stars packed in spherical form, and look like hazy mothballs when viewed through small telescopes. *Planetary nebulae* are gas surrounding a dying star and *diffuse nebulae* are clouds of gas and dust in space. *Galaxies* are giant systems of billions of stars, gas, and dust. A few of these non-stellar objects are named on the star maps.

You will notice that some star clusters on the maps have names that consist of M and a number, such as M13. M13 is the globular cluster in Hercules that can be seen with the naked eye (see p. 60); it is also the thirteenth object on a list compiled over 200 years ago by an astronomer named Charles Messier. Messier made a list of about 100 objects that looked fuzzy in the sky, so that he would not misidentify them as he searched for comets. We now use his list to name many interesting objects in the sky; most, however, can be seen only with binoculars or a telescope.

The ecliptic, shown on the maps as a dotted line, marks the path of the sun and the approximate path of the planets in the sky. The planets will always be found close to this imaginary line across the sky.

LEGEND-KEY

STELLAR MAGNITUDES:

-1  0  1  2  3  4

● • DOUBLE STARS

⊙ ∘ VARIABLE STARS

○ OPEN STAR CLUSTER

⊕ GLOBULAR STAR CLUSTER

✧ PLANETARY NEBULA

□ DIFFUSE NEBULA

⊘ GALAXY

SPECTRAL TYPE (Brightest stars only)

O,B  A  F  G  K  M

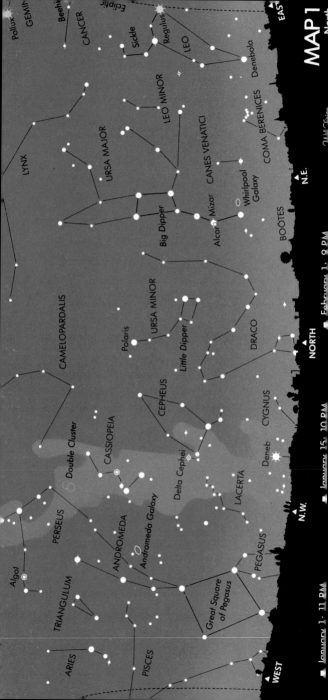

MAP 1
North

■ January 1 · 11 PM   ■ January 15 · 10 PM   ■ February 1 · 9 PM

WEST   N.W.   NORTH   N.E.   EAST

Constellations and features labeled: Pollux, GEMINI, Beehive, CANCER, Sickle, Regulus, LEO, Denebola, Ecliptic, LYNX, URSA MAJOR, LEO MINOR, CANES VENATICI, COMA BERENICES, Big Dipper, Alcor, Mizar, Whirlpool Galaxy, BOÖTES, CAMELOPARDALIS, URSA MINOR, Polaris, Little Dipper, DRACO, CEPHEUS, Double Cluster, CASSIOPEIA, Delta Cephei, CYGNUS, Deneb, LACERTA, PERSEUS, Algol, ANDROMEDA, Andromeda Galaxy, TRIANGULUM, PEGASUS, Great Square of Pegasus, ARIES, PISCES

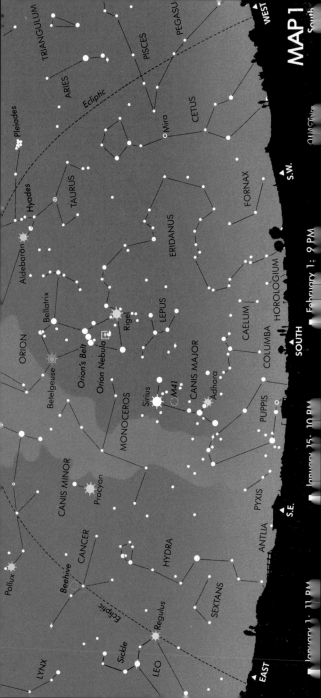

MAP 1

WEST

South

S.W.

February 1: 9 PM

SOUTH

January 15: 10 PM

S.E.

January 1: 11 PM

EAST

TRIANGULUM

PEGASUS

PISCES

ARIES

Ecliptic

Pleiades

Hyades

TAURUS

Aldebaran

Bellatrix

ORION

Orion's Belt

Betelgeuse

Orion Nebula

Rigel

CETUS

Mira

FORNAX

ERIDANUS

LEPUS

CAELUM

COLUMBA

HOROLOGIUM

CANIS MAJOR

Sirius

M41

Adhara

MONOCEROS

PUPPIS

PYXIS

ANTLIA

CANIS MINOR

Procyon

CANCER

Beehive

HYDRA

SEXTANS

Pollux

LYNX

Ecliptic

Regulus

Sickle

LEO

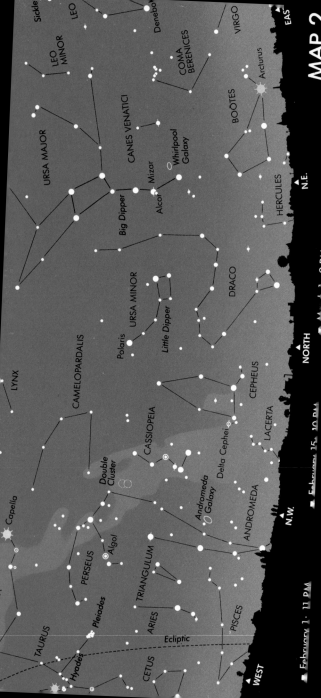

MAP 2

Sickle  LEO  LEO MINOR  Denebola  VIRGO  COMA BERENICES  Arcturus  BOÖTES  HERCULES

URSA MAJOR  CANES VENATICI  Whirlpool Galaxy  Mizar  Alcor  Big Dipper

DRACO  URSA MINOR  Polaris  Little Dipper  CAMELOPARDALIS

CEPHEUS  LACERTA  CASSIOPEIA  Double Cluster  Delta Cephei  Andromeda Galaxy  ANDROMEDA

LYNX  Capella  PERSEUS  Algol  TRIANGULUM  ARIES  PISCES

TAURUS  Pleiades  Hyades  Ecliptic  CETUS

February 1 · 11 P.M.
February 15 · 10 P.M.

EAS  N.E.  NORTH  N.W.  WEST

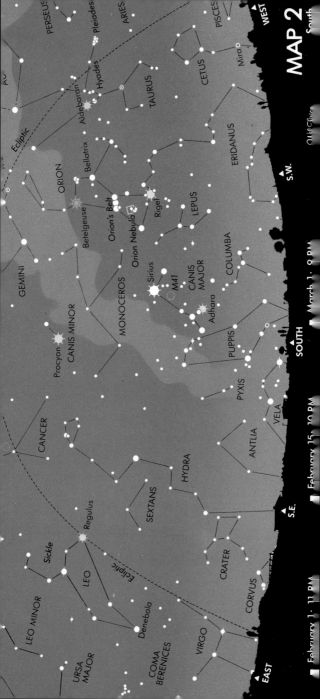

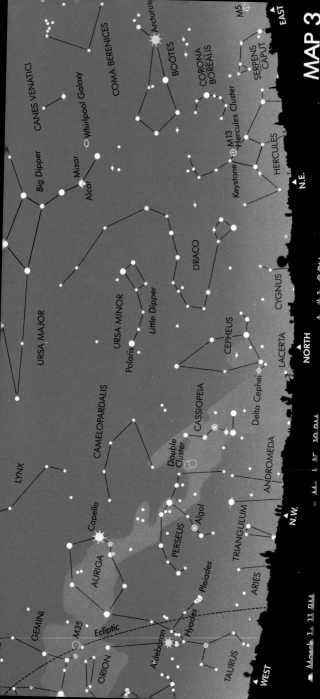

**MAP 3**

EAST

M5

SERPENS CAPUT

CORONA BOREALIS

BOÖTES

Arcturus

COMA BERENICES

Hercules Cluster

M13

HERCULES

Keystone

N.E.

CANES VENATICI

Whirlpool Galaxy

Big Dipper

Mizar
Alcor

DRACO

CYGNUS

NORTH

URSA MAJOR

URSA MINOR

Little Dipper

Polaris

CEPHEUS

LACERTA

CAMELOPARDALIS

Double Cluster

CASSIOPEIA

Delta Cephei

ANDROMEDA

LYNX

Capella

AURIGA

PERSEUS

Algol

N.W.

TRIANGULUM

GEMINI

M35

ARIES

Ecliptic

Hyades

Pleiades

ORION

Aldebaran

TAURUS

WEST

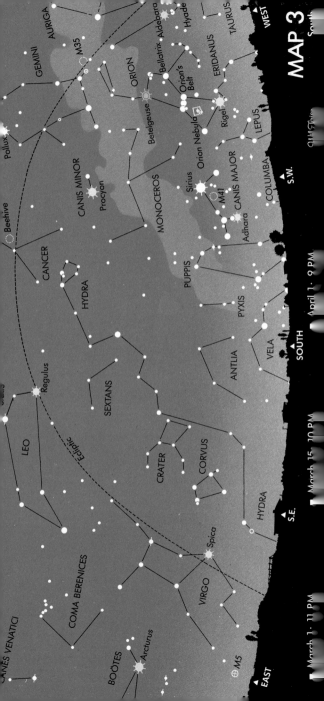

MAP 3

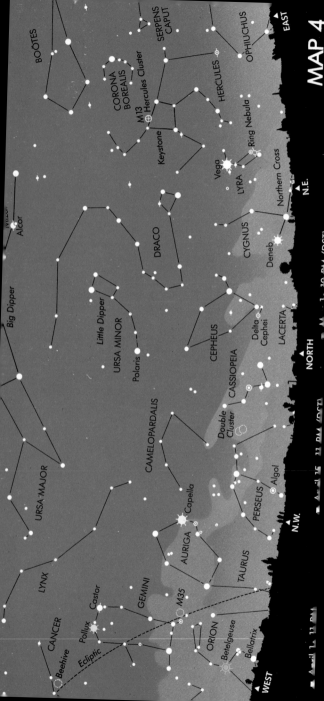

MAP 4

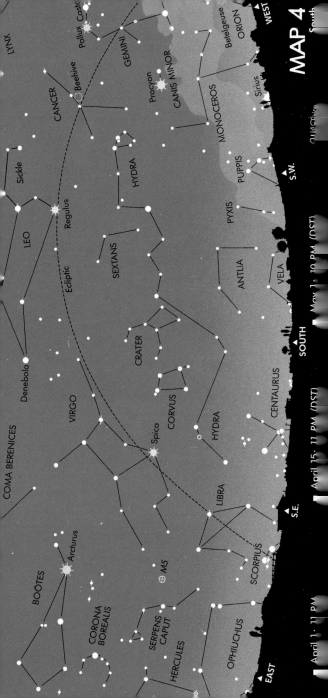

MAP 4

South

WEST

LYNX

Pollux Castor

GEMINI

Beehive

CANCER

Procyon

CANIS MINOR

Betelgeuse

ORION

Sirius

Sickle

CANCER

MONOCEROS

Regulus

LEO

HYDRA

PUPPIS

S.W.

Denebola

Ecliptic

SEXTANS

PYXIS

COMA BERENICES

VIRGO

CRATER

ANTLIA

VELA

May 1, 10 PM (DST)

SOUTH

Spica

CORVUS

HYDRA

CENTAURUS

April 15, 11 PM (DST)

Arcturus

LIBRA

S.E.

BOÖTES

⊕ M5

SCORPIUS

CORONA
BOREALIS

SERPENS
CAPUT

OPHIUCHUS

HERCULES

EAST

April 1, 11 PM

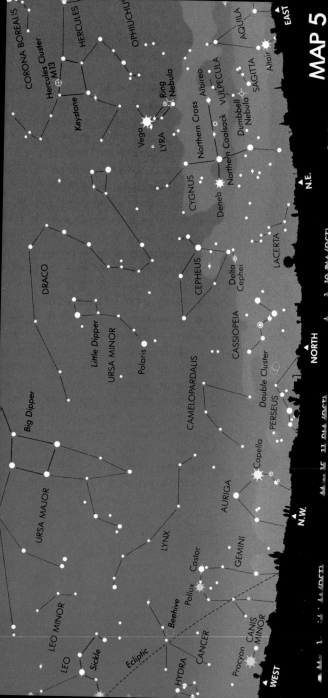

MAP 5

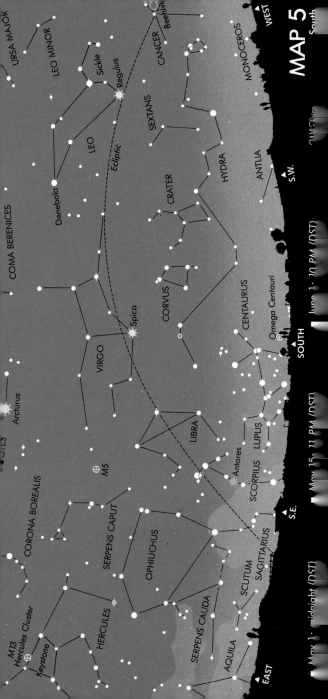

MAP 5

South

WEST

S.W.

SOUTH

S.E.

EAST

July 1 · 9 PM (DST)

June 1 · 10 PM (DST)

May 15 · 11 PM (DST)

May 1 · midnight (DST)

URSA MAJOR

LEO MINOR

Sickle

Regulus

CANCER

Beehive

MONOCEROS

LEO

Ecliptic

SEXTANS

Denebola

HYDRA

ANTLIA

COMA BERENICES

CRATER

CORVUS

CENTAURUS

Spica

Omega Centauri

VIRGO

Arcturus

LIBRA

LUPUS

CORONA BOREALIS

M5

Antares

SCORPIUS

SERPENS CAPUT

OPHIUCHUS

SCUTUM

SAGITTARIUS

HERCULES

M13
Hercules Cluster

Keystone

SERPENS CAUDA

AQUILA

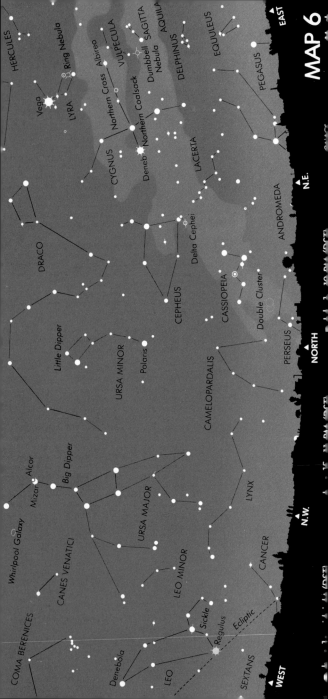

# MAP 6

**EAST**

HERCULES

Ring Nebula

Vega

LYRA

Albireo

Northern Cross

VULPECULA

SAGITTA

AQUILA

Dumbbell Nebula

Deneb

Northern Coalsack

DELPHINUS

CYGNUS

EQUULEUS

LACERTA

PEGASUS

**N.E.**

DRACO

Delta Cephei

ANDROMEDA

CEPHEUS

CASSIOPEIA

Double Cluster

Little Dipper

URSA MINOR

Polaris

PERSEUS

**NORTH**

CAMELOPARDALIS

Big Dipper

Alcor

Mizar

URSA MAJOR

LYNX

**N.W.**

Whirlpool Galaxy

CANES VENATICI

LEO MINOR

CANCER

COMA BERENICES

Sickle

Regulus

Ecliptic

Denebola

LEO

SEXTANS

**WEST**

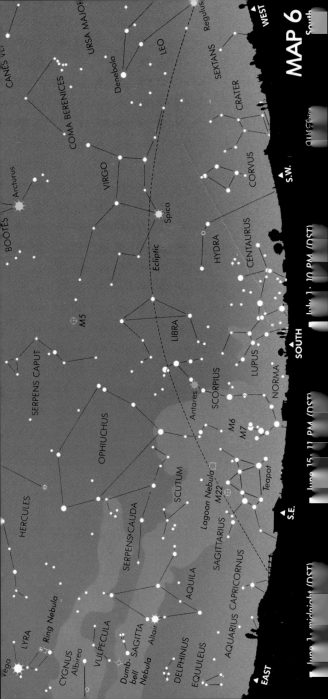

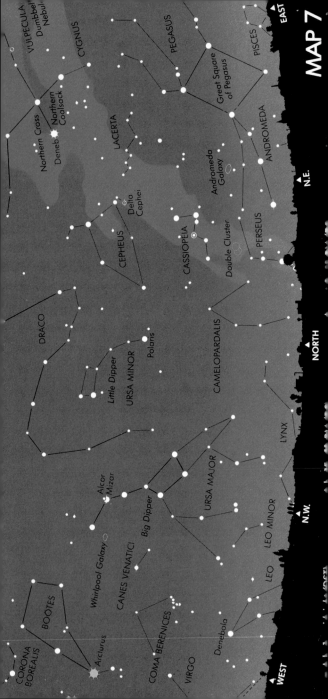

MAP 7

EAST

PISCES

PEGASUS

Great Square
of Pegasus

VULPECULA
Dumbbell
Nebula

CYGNUS

ANDROMEDA

Northern Cross

Deneb

Northern
Coalsack

LACERTA

Andromeda
Galaxy

N.E.

Delta
Cephei

PERSEUS

CEPHEUS

CASSIOPEIA

Double Cluster

DRACO

CAMELOPARDALIS

NORTH

Little Dipper

URSA MINOR

Polaris

LYNX

Alcor
Mizar

URSA MAJOR

N.W.

Big Dipper

LEO MINOR

Whirlpool Galaxy

BOOTES

CANES VENATICI

LEO

CORONA
BOREALIS

COMA BERENICES

Denebola

Arcturus

VIRGO

WEST

BOÖTES

CORONA
BOREALIS

Arcturus

COMA BERENICES

VIRGO

Spica

M5

LIBRA

HYDRA

SERPENS CAPUT

LUPUS

OPHIUCHUS

Antares

SCORPIUS

NORMA

M6

M7

Lagoon
Nebula

M22

Teapot

SERPENS CAUDA

SCUTUM

SAGITTARIUS

CORONA
AUSTRALIS

Ecliptic

AQUILA

Altair

CAPRICORNUS

MICROSCOPIUM

VULPECULA

SAGITTA

Northern Cross

DELPHINUS

EQUULEUS

Dumbbell
Nebula

AQUARIUS

CYGNUS

PEGASUS

PISCES

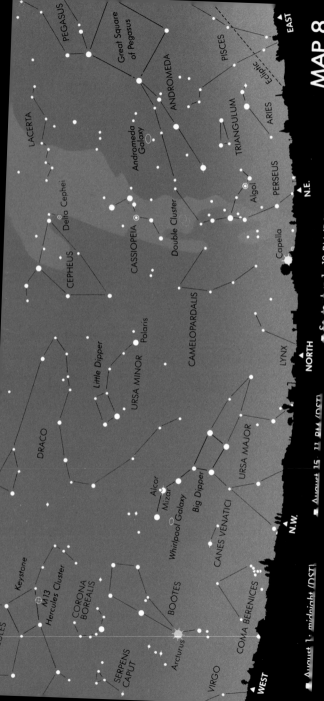

MAP 8

■ August 1, midnight (DST)

■ August 15, 11 P.M. (DST)

■ September 15, 10 P.M. (DST)

EAST

N.E.

NORTH

N.W.

WEST

PEGASUS

Great Square
of Pegasus

PISCES

Ecliptic

ANDROMEDA

LACERTA

Andromeda
Galaxy

TRIANGULUM

ARIES

Delta Cephei

CASSIOPEIA

Double Cluster

Algol

PERSEUS

CEPHEUS

Capella

CAMELOPARDALIS

Little Dipper

Polaris

URSA MINOR

LYNX

DRACO

Alcor

Mizar

Whirlpool Galaxy

Big Dipper

URSA MAJOR

CANES VENATICI

Keystone

M13
Hercules Cluster

CORONA
BOREALIS

BOOTES

COMA BERENICES

SERPENS
CAPUT

Arcturus

VIRGO

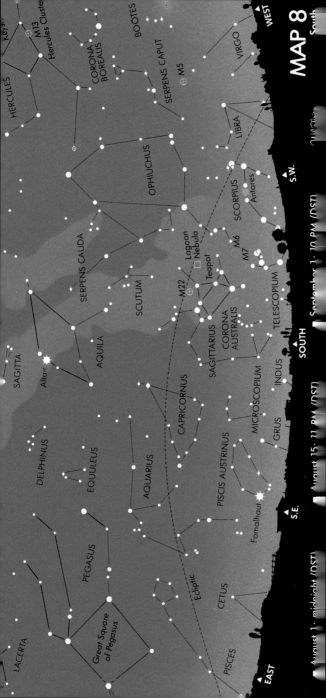

MAP 8

WEST

South

VIRGO

BOÖTES

CORONA
BOREALIS

⊕ M5

SERPENS CAPUT

Keys.

M13
Hercules Cluster

HERCULES

LIBRA

Old Giza

⊙

OPHIUCHUS

SCORPIUS

Antares

S.W.

SERPENS CAUDA

Lagoon
Nebula

M6

M7

M22 ⊕

Teapot

TELESCOPIUM

September 1: 10 PM (DST)

SCUTUM

SAGITTARIUS

CORONA
AUSTRALIS

SOUTH

AQUILA

SAGITTA

Altair

INDUS

CAPRICORNUS

MICROSCOPIUM

DELPHINUS

EQUULEUS

GRUS

August 15: 11 PM (DST)

S.E.

AQUARIUS

PISCIS AUSTRINUS

Fomalhaut

PEGASUS

LACERTA

Great Square
of Pegasus

Ecliptic

CETUS

August 1: midnight (DST)

PISCES

EAST

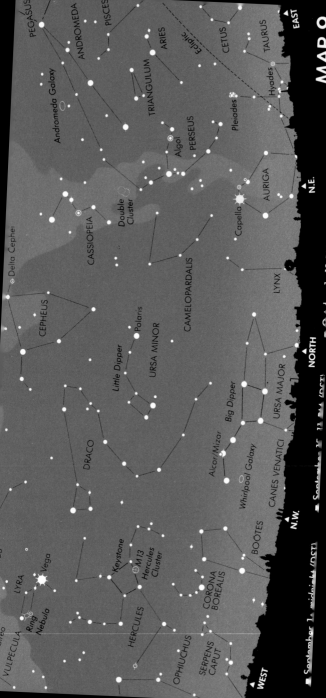

MAP 9

September 1, 11 P.M. (DST)
September 16, midnight (DST)

**EAST**

**N.E.**

**NORTH**

**N.W.**

**WEST**

PEGASUS
ANDROMEDA
PISCES
ARIES
TRIANGULUM
CETUS
TAURUS
Hyades
Pleiades
Andromeda Galaxy
Algol
PERSEUS
AURIGA
Capella
Double Cluster
CASSIOPEIA
CAMELOPARDALIS
LYNX
CEPHEUS
Delta Cephei
Polaris
Little Dipper
URSA MINOR
DRACO
Big Dipper
URSA MAJOR
Alcor/Mizar
Whirlpool Galaxy
CANES VENATICI
BOOTES
Keystone
M13
Hercules Cluster
CORONA BOREALIS
Vega
LYRA
Ring Nebula
VULPECULA
HERCULES
SERPENS CAPUT
OPHIUCHUS

Ecliptic

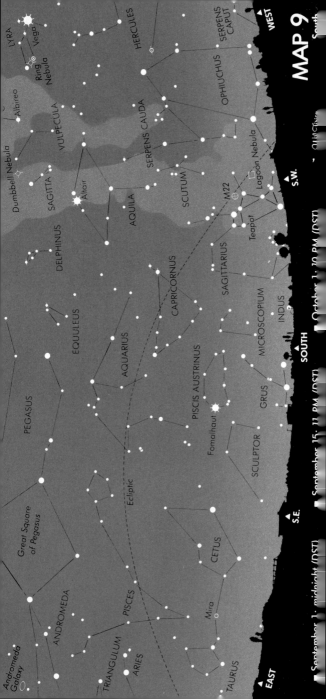

MAP 9

WEST

SOUTH

EAST

S.W.

S.E.

South

Quadreine

October 1, 10 PM (DST)

September 15, 11 PM (DST)

September 1, midnight (DST)

LYRA
Vega
Ring Nebula
Albireo
HERCULES
SERPENS CAPUT
OPHIUCHUS
SERPENS CAUDA
VULPECULA
Dumbbell Nebula
SAGITTA
Altair
AQUILA
SCUTUM
M22
Lagoon Nebula
Teapot
DELPHINUS
CAPRICORNUS
SAGITTARIUS
MICROSCOPIUM
INDUS
EQUULEUS
AQUARIUS
PEGASUS
Ecliptic
Great Square of Pegasus
PISCIS AUSTRINUS
Fomalhaut
GRUS
SCULPTOR
ANDROMEDA
Andromeda Galaxy
PISCES
TRIANGULUM
ARIES
CETUS
Mira
TAURUS

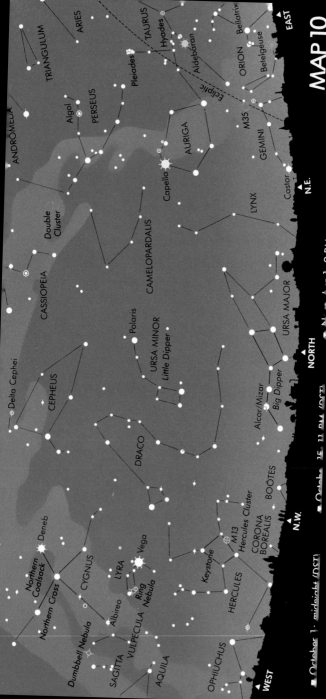

MAP 10

EAST

Bellatrix
ORION
Betelgeuse
Aldebaran
Hyades
TAURUS
Ecliptic
M35
GEMINI
Castor

N.E.

Pleiades
ARIES
TRIANGULUM
Algol
PERSEUS
ANDROMEDA
AURIGA
Capella
LYNX

Double
Cluster
CASSIOPEIA
CAMELOPARDALIS
URSA MAJOR

Delta Cephei
CEPHEUS
Polaris
URSA MINOR
Little Dipper
DRACO

NORTH

Big Dipper
Alcor/Mizar

Deneb
Northern Coalsack
CYGNUS
Northern Cross
Albireo
VULPECULA
Dumbbell Nebula
SAGITTA
AQUILA
OPHIUCHUS

N.W.

BOOTES

LYRA
Vega
Ring Nebula
M13
Hercules Cluster
CORONA
BOREALIS
Keystone
HERCULES

WEST

October 1: midnight (DST)
October 15: 11 PM (DST)
November 1: 9 PM

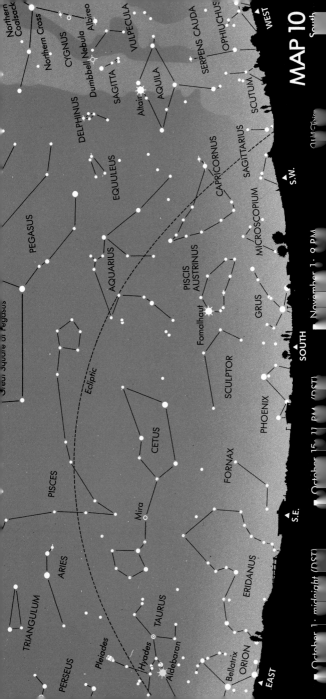

MAP 10

WEST

South

S.W.

November 1 · 9 PM

SOUTH

October 15 · 11 PM (PST)

S.E.

October 1 · midnight (DST)

EAST

Northern Coalsack

Northern Cross

CYGNUS

Albireo

Dumbbell Nebula

SAGITTA

DELPHINIUS

Altair

AQUILA

VULPECULA

SERPENS CAUDA

OPHIUCHUS

SCUTUM

SAGITTARIUS

CAPRICORNUS

EQUULEUS

PEGASUS

Great Square of Pegasus

AQUARIUS

Ecliptic

MICROSCOPIUM

PISCIS AUSTRINUS

Fomalhaut

GRUS

SCULPTOR

PHOENIX

FORNAX

PISCES

CETUS

Mira

TRIANGULUM

ARIES

PERSEUS

Pleiades

Hyades

TAURUS

Aldebaran

Bellatrix

ORION

ERIDANUS

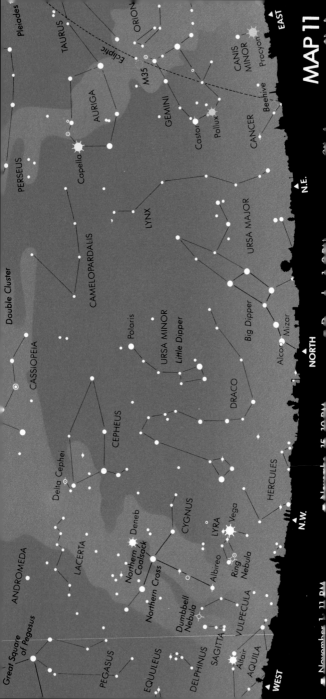

MAP 11

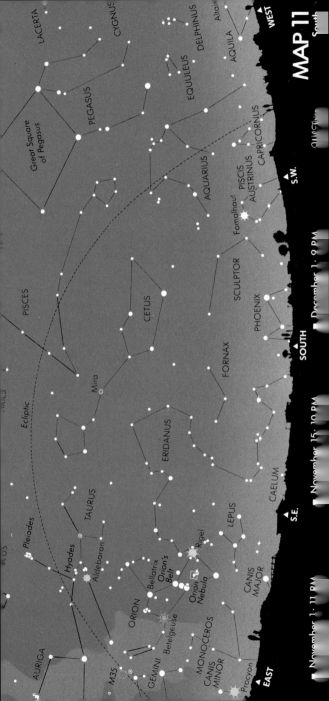

MAP 11

WEST
South
S.W.
SOUTH
S.E.
EAST

LACERTA
CYGNUS
PEGASUS
Great Square of Pegasus
DELPHINUS
EQUULEUS
AQUILA
Altair
CAPRICORNUS
AQUARIUS
PISCES
PISCIS AUSTRINUS
Fomalhaut
SCULPTOR
PHOENIX
CETUS
Mira
FORNAX
ERIDANUS
CAELUM
LEPUS
PISCES
Ecliptic
TAURUS
Pleiades
Hyades
Aldebaran
ORION
Bellatrix
Orion's Belt
Rigel
Orion Nebula
Betelgeuse
CANIS MAJOR
MONOCEROS
AURIGA
M35
GEMINI
CANIS MINOR
Procyon

December 1, 9 PM
November 15, 10 PM
November 1, 11 PM

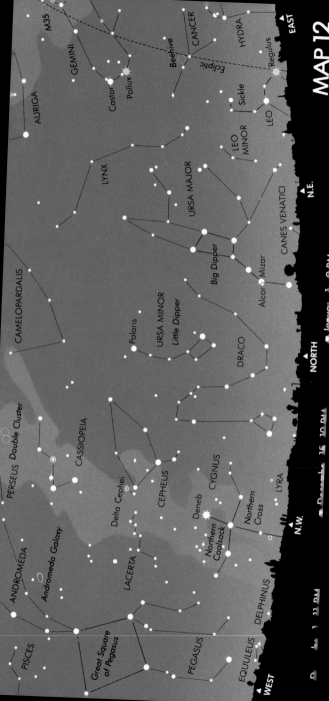

MAP 12

EAST

HYDRA

CANCER

Beehive

Ecliptic

Regulus

Sickle

LEO

LEO
MINOR

N.E.

CANES VENATICI

URSA MAJOR

Big Dipper

Alcor & Mizar

DRACO

NORTH

M35

GEMINI

Castor

Pollux

AURIGA

LYNX

URSA MINOR
Little Dipper

Polaris

CAMELOPARDALIS

CEPHEUS

CASSIOPEIA

Delta Cephei

PERSEUS Double Cluster

ANDROMEDA

Andromeda Galaxy

PISCES

Great Square
of Pegasus

PEGASUS

EQUULEUS

DELPHINUS

LYRA

CYGNUS

Northern
Cross

Northern
Coalsack

Deneb

LACERTA

N.W.

WEST

December 15 10 PM

January 1 9 PM

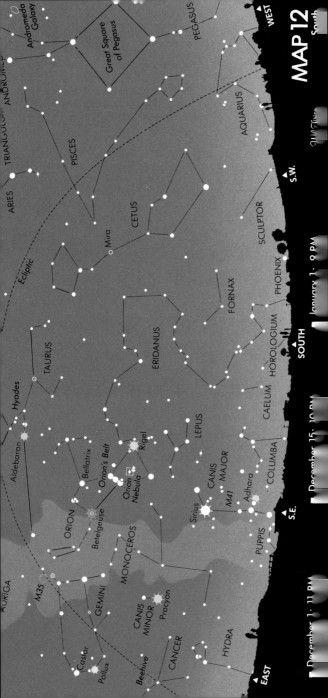

# Meet the Constellations

## URSA MAJOR, URSA MINOR

Ursa Major and Ursa Minor, the Big Bear and the Little Bear, are two of the most familiar constellations. For those of us at midnorthern latitudes, they can be seen during all seasons.

In a Greek myth, Zeus, king of the gods, fell in love with Callisto. Together they had a son, Arcas. Zeus, in one story, changed Callisto into a bear to protect her from the jealousy of his wife, Hera. When Arcas grew up, he almost shot his mother by mistake. Zeus protected Callisto by changing Arcas into another bear and by placing both bears in the sky. He carried them up by their tails, which explains why the bears in the sky have such long tails. Hera, in her jealousy, convinced the sea-god Poseidon not to let the bears bathe in the sea. Indeed, Ursa Major and Ursa Minor are always above the horizon and thus visible in the sky at night.

The Big Dipper and the Little Dipper make up only parts of the constellations Ursa Major and Ursa Minor, so they are considered asterisms (see p. 10) rather than constellations. The star in the middle of the Big Dipper's handle is a double star, as you can see with the naked eye if your eyesight is good. The brighter of the two stars is known as Mizar, and the fainter one is Alcor. The Native Americans called them a horse and rider. In a telescope, Mizar turns out to be double itself.

Follow the Pointers of the Big Dipper to Polaris, the North Star, which is at the end of the handle of the Little Dipper. Polaris is the closest bright star to the celestial north pole, only about 1° away from it (twice the diameter of the moon, or half the width of your thumb at the end of your outstretched arm). Polaris orbits the pole once a day. The other stars in the Little Dipper between Polaris and the end of the bowl are hard to see.

## ORION

The constellation Orion, visible on winter evenings, is one of the easiest to find in the sky. Three stars of about the same brightness appear in a straight line and form Orion's belt. You can spot them easily when scanning the sky. The reddish star Betelgeuse is about 9° to one side of the belt and the bluish star Rigel is about an equal distance to the other side of the belt. Betelgeuse is a cool supergiant star, one of the largest stars known. Rigel is a hot star.

In Greek mythology, Orion was a hunter. The sun-god Apollo was afraid that Orion would take advantage of his sister Artemis, the goddess of the hunt. Apollo sent Scorpius, the Scorpion, to attack Orion, who escaped by leaping into the sea. Apollo then tricked his sister into shooting at a dark spot on the waves; her arrow hit Orion, who died. Artemis could not have Orion revived, but placed him in the heavens, where the scorpion still pursues him. (See Maps 1–3, 11, and 12, facing south.)

In the sky, we see Orion's sword hanging from his belt. A hazy region in the sword, readily visible through binoculars, is the nebula shown below. Deep inside this cloud of glowing gas is a stellar nursery where stars are being born.

The Orion Nebula, glowing gas in Orion's sword.

## CASSIOPEIA

Cassiopeia was Queen of Ethiopia, married to King Cepheus. The boastful queen claimed that she was more beautiful than the sea nymphs. The nymphs had Neptune, king of the sea, punish Cassiopeia by having the whale Cetus rampage through the kingdom. An oracle said that only the sacrifice of Princess Andromeda, daughter of Cepheus and Cassiopeia, to Cetus would save the kingdom.

All the characters in this tale are visible in the sky. Cassiopeia is marked by its W-shape in the sky, with stars ranging from magnitude 2 to 3.5 marking each turn in the W. (Cassiopeia appears on all the northern star maps.)

Cassiopeia lies in the Milky Way, so many nebulae (clouds of gas and dust) and star clusters lie within it. Scanning Cassiopeia with binoculars will reveal many of them.

In the year 1572, a bright new star appeared in Cassiopeia. It was bright enough to shine even during the daytime for a few weeks. This object was a supernova, a star that exploded (see p. 74). Only faint traces of the supernova remain visible. In the photo below, images of radio waves were used to show the circular shell of gas thrown out by a more recent supernova.

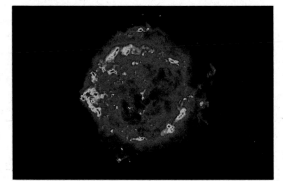

This image shows radio waves coming from the site of the supernova explosion that took place in Cassiopeia in the late 17th century. The remnant's size in the sky is one-quarter the diameter of the moon.

## ANDROMEDA

When we left Cassiopeia, the gods had demanded the sacrifice of her daughter Andromeda to save the kingdom. Andromeda was chained to a rock at the edge of the sea, about to be attacked by the whale Cetus. Fortunately, Perseus arrived and turned Cetus into stone by showing him the head of Medusa, a monster he had just killed (see p. 52).

In the sky, the constellation Andromeda is next to Cassiopeia (see Maps 1–3 and 7–10, facing north; it is too near the zenith to show on Maps 11 and 12). Perseus is next to Andromeda.

In the middle of Andromeda, you can see a faint hazy patch of light if the night is dark. This patch is the Great Galaxy of Andromeda, also known as M31 in Messier's catalogue, a list of star clusters. It is a spiral of a trillion stars plus gas and dust; our own Milky Way Galaxy is thought to look much like it. The Great Galaxy in Andromeda is over 2 million light-years away; that means that the light we see from it has been traveling to us for over 2 million years. This galaxy and one other are the most distant things in the universe that you can see with the naked eye.

The Great Galaxy of Andromeda, M31, a spiral galaxy. Its two companion galaxies also show clearly in this photo. All are behind the many foreground stars in our own galaxy.

## PERSEUS

Perseus, in Greek mythology, was helped by the goddess Athena, who gave him a shield so polished that you could see reflections in it. Perseus was sent off to kill the sisters known as the Gorgons, winged monsters so horrible that all who looked at them turned into stone. Perseus managed to cut off the head of Medusa, one of the Gorgons, without looking in her direction: he used Medusa's reflection in Athena's shield to aim his sword. Thus he was not turned into stone. Perseus saved Andromeda, chained to a rock, by showing Medusa's head to the whale Cetus and turning him into stone (see p. 50).

In the sky, Perseus is at the side of Andromeda along the Milky Way. They are high in the sky on a winter evening. If you use binoculars, you can see a pair of open star clusters close together in the midst of the Milky Way in Perseus. This double cluster is shown below.

Another remarkable object in Perseus is the variable star Algol. Every 2.9 days, Algol becomes fainter than its normal brightness for a period of five hours. It goes from its normal magnitude of 2.2 down to magnitude 3.5 and back to magnitude 2.2 again. It does so when one of the stars in the Algol double-star system goes in front of the brighter one.

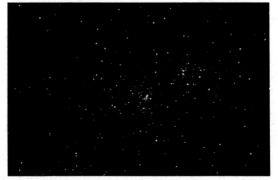

The double cluster in Perseus, a pair of open clusters. The stars in these clusters are very young.

# PEGASUS

When Perseus killed Medusa with his sword, the winged horse Pegasus arose from Medusa's blood. Pegasus was wild, and the hero Bellerophon had to tame him. Bellerophon's various successes had made him vain, and he tried to ride Pegasus up to the gods' home in Olympus. The gods were angered by his presumption, and Zeus, the king of the gods, sent a gadfly to sting Pegasus. The horse threw Bellerophon, who was severely injured, but Pegasus continued up to Mt. Olympus and the stars.

In the sky, Pegasus is marked by "the Great Square of Pegasus"—four stars in the horse's body that form a square whose sides are each over 10° (the width of one fist, held up to the sky) across. You can find the Great Square of Pegasus by following the line from the Pointers of the Big Dipper through Polaris and then twice as far on Polaris' other side. One of the stars is actually now over the boundary into the constellation Andromeda—see Maps 1, 7, and 8 (facing north); 10 (facing south); 11, and 12. The other three stars are in Pegasus proper. All are between 2nd and 3rd magnitude. There are no brighter stars in the square.

M15, a globular cluster in Pegasus, visible only with binoculars or a telescope. It is the fifteenth object on Messier's list (see p. 19).

## TAURUS

In Greek mythology, Taurus, the Bull, was Zeus himself. He disguised himself as a white bull in order to attract the attention of Europa, Princess of Phoenicia. Europa found the bull so attractive that she climbed on his back, and Zeus swam off with her.

In the sky, Taurus is charging at Orion (see Maps 1–3 and 10–12, facing south). Only the front part of a bull appears as the constellation in the sky. The head of Taurus is clearly marked by the V-shape of an open star cluster, the Hyades. The bright reddish star Aldebaran marks one of the bull's eyes.

The Pleiades, another open cluster, ride on the Bull's back. With a little training, your eyes can readily pick up the Pleiades as you scan the sky. The Pleiades are called the seven sisters in Greek mythology. Six of the Pleiades stars are about 4th magnitude and so are easy to see with the naked eye, but some people can see at least two other, fainter stars. Binoculars or a telescope will reveal dozens of Pleiades stars, as the picture below shows.

The Pleiades; about six of them are visible to the naked eye. Atlas and above it, Pleione, are the two brightest stars at left. Alcyone is in the center of the picture. Continuing counterclockwise around the diamond are Merope, Electra, and Maia. The stars are young, and in some cases are still surrounded by some of the dust from which they formed.

## CYGNUS

Cygnus was a friend of the youth Phaethon. Though Phaethon was mortal, his father was Helius, the sun god, who supposedly carried the sun across the sky each day in his chariot. Phaethon beseeched his father to let him drive the chariot one day. But Phaethon drove recklessly and lost control. Zeus had to save the Earth from the sun's heat by hurling a thunderbolt at the chariot. Phaethon fell into a river and Cygnus, his friend, plunged in to search for him. Helius changed Cygnus into a swan and placed him in the sky.

In the sky, the constellation Cygnus lies along the Milky Way (Maps 4–7 and 9–12, facing north; it is too high to appear on northern Map 8). Its brightest stars mark the Northern Cross. Cygnus, with the bright star Deneb in the swan's tail, appears high in the summer sky. The three bright stars Deneb, Vega (in the constellation Lyra), and Altair (in the constellation Aquila) mark the Summer Triangle. Altair is about 40° from Deneb and Vega.

Albireo, the bright star at the head of the Northern Cross and of Cygnus, is a very pretty double star. With binoculars, you can see that it consists of two stars of different colors.

The Milky Way in Cygnus includes the Northern Cross.

## HERCULES

Hercules was the most famous of the Greek heroes. In mythology, he was the son of Zeus, king of the gods, and of Perseus' granddaughter. Zeus' ever-jealous wife, Hera, prevented Hercules from assuming his rightful place on the throne, and even sent two serpents to kill him in his crib. The infant Hercules strangled the serpents. Later, he was forced to serve another king, who ordered him to perform 12 great labors. In the first of the labors, he slew a lion (see Leo, p. 62), and wore its skin thereafter. His other labors included cleaning the stables of King Augeas in a single day, bringing back golden apples from a garden guarded by a dragon, and bringing the three-headed dog Cerberus up from guarding the gates of the lower world. Hercules died on a funeral pyre, which consumed his body and sent his spirit to Olympus.

Four stars in the middle of the constellation Hercules form an asterism known as the Keystone (see Maps 3–5 and 8–10, facing north). In the middle of one of its sides, a globular-type star cluster (see p. 73) known as M13 or the Globular Cluster in Hercules is found. It is barely visible as a faint patch of light to the naked eye, and looks like a mothball when seen through binoculars or a small telescope. The cluster contains about 100,000 stars packed into a relatively small space.

The most prominent globular cluster in the northern sky, M13 in Hercules.

## LEO

In Greek mythology, Leo was the ferocious lion that Hercules slew in the first of his labors (see p. 60).

In the sky, you can find Leo by following the back two stars of the Big Dipper's bowl in the opposite direction from that of the Pointers to Polaris. About twice as far along as Polaris is from the Pointers, you come to the bright star Regulus. Regulus marks the dot at the bottom of the backward question mark known as the Sickle. The rest of Leo spreads out behind the Sickle (see Maps 1, 2; 3 and 4, facing south; 5 and 6; 7 and 12, facing north). Leo is highest in the sky at sunset during the winter and spring.

Each year, around November 17, the Earth passes through the path of an old comet. As the comet dust burns up in the Earth's atmosphere, we see the Leonid meteor shower, meteors that appear to come from the constellation Leo. The dust is bunched in space  and every 33 years we see a spectacular Leonid shower. The last spectacular shower, shown below, took place in 1966, so we expect another fabulous event in 1998 or 1999.

Meteors of the exceptionally strong Leonid meteor shower in 1966 appear to come from the constellation Leo (note the Sickle) as they streak across the sky during this time exposure. Because the shutter was open for more than 3 minutes, the star images are trailed. Two of the meteors appear as points because they were coming straight at the camera.

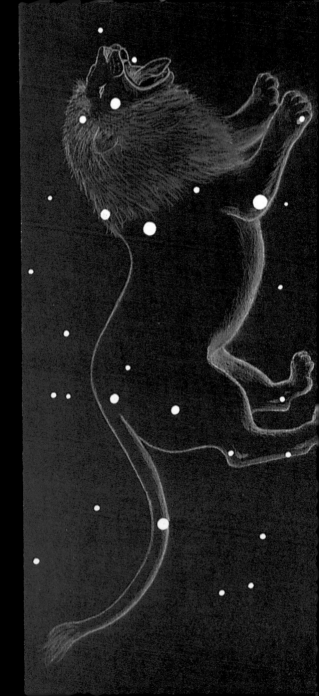

## CANIS MAJOR

Canis Major, the Big Dog, is often identified as Orion's companion. In the sky, it is next to Orion (see Maps 1–3 and 11–12, facing south). Canis Major is also ready to pounce on Lepus, the Rabbit, one of the animals that Orion hunted.

Sirius, the Dog Star, is the brightest star in Canis Major. It is easy to find, both because it is the brightest star in the sky and because Orion's belt points to it. If Orion is upright, with Betelgeuse at the top, follow the belt to your left.

In August, Sirius becomes visible for the first time each year well after midnight, before the sun brightens the morning sky. This yearly event has given the sultry "dog days" of summer their name.

About 4° (two fingers' width) south of Sirius, in Canis Major, the open star cluster known as M41 (the 41st object in Messier's catalogue) appears. Like all open clusters, it contains a few hundred young stars and has no particular shape. Together the stars are just bright enough to be seen with the naked eye. With binoculars or a telescope, they make a beautiful view, covering about as much sky as the full moon does.

Sirius is significant for astronomers because around it orbits a much smaller star, known as Sirius B. Sirius B was the first "white dwarf" star (see p. 74) to be discovered.

M41, an open cluster in Canis Major.

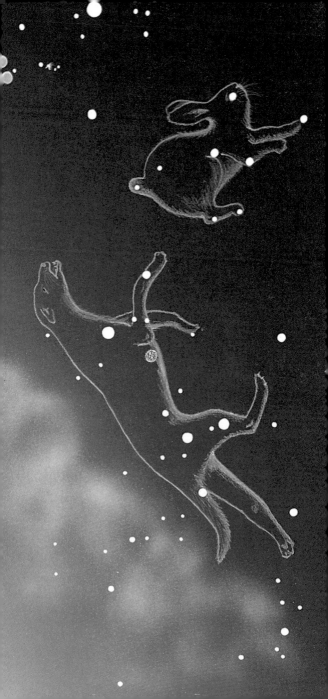

## SAGITTARIUS

Sagittarius, in Greek mythology, is not only an archer but also a centaur, half-human and half-horse. Sometimes Sagittarius is identified as Chiron, the wisest centaur.

In the sky, Sagittarius (Maps 5–10) is marked by an asterism known as the Teapot, found near the archer's bow and arrow. Sagittarius appears best on a summer evening, though it never becomes high in the sky for us. Both the ecliptic— the path where you will find the planets— and the Milky Way go through it. The center of our galaxy is in the direction of the constellation Sagittarius, so the densest part of the Milky Way is there. Thus in Sagittarius we find many nebulae and star clusters. In the Lagoon Nebula shown below (M8 in Messier's catalogue), we see glowing gas given energy by embedded stars. The nebula is crossed by dark gas, which forms the lagoon that can be seen with binoculars or a telescope. The Lagoon Nebula is barely visible to the naked eye as a hazy white region about as large as the full moon.

Within a few degrees of the Lagoon Nebula lie several other beautiful nebulae and star clusters. Scanning this region of the sky with binoculars can be fun.

The Lagoon Nebula in Sagittarius. Dark dust that absorbs light from behind it makes the lagoon we see in this photo. From the rest of the nebula, we get the reddish light given off by hydrogen gas. The red color shows up only in photographs, when the film is exposed for several minutes.

## When to See Different Constellations

The Earth rotates on its axis once every day
and it revolves around the sun once each year.
But how do we measure rotation? Astronomers measure the length of a day in two ways:
with respect to the sun and with respect to the
stars. Measurements with respect to the stars
are called *sidereal* (sye-dee'ree-al).

When the Earth has rotated once with
respect to the sun, one ordinary (solar) day has
passed. When the Earth has rotated once with
respect to the stars, it has also moved ahead
$\frac{1}{365}$ of the distance around its orbit (since
there are 365 days in a year). The Earth must
then rotate a little farther before an observer
on Earth sees the sun come back to the same
place in the sky. In fact, it must rotate an additional $\frac{1}{365}$ of a day, which is 3 minutes 56 seconds. Thus a solar day is longer than a
sidereal day by 3 minutes 56 seconds.

As a result, constellations rise nearly 4 minutes earlier each day. When a month has
passed, they rise about 30 days $\times$ 4 minutes
per day = 120 minutes = 2 hours earlier. This
difference is shown on the star maps (pp. 20–
43). We thus see different constellations in
each season.

If we were at the north pole, we would always
see the northern constellations and never the
southern ones. If we were at the equator, we
would see all the constellations, both northern
and southern, but each constellation would be
"up" for only half the time. We are at latitudes
approximately midway between the equator
and the north pole, so some constellations—
the *circumpolar* ones—are always in view—
while others are "up"—above the horizon—
during the nighttime only part of the time.

Though circumpolar constellations are
always in the sky, sometimes they are above
the celestial north pole and sometimes they are
below it. These constellations will be higher in
the sky, and thus usually easier to see, when
they are above the celestial north pole.

# Circumpolar Constellations (from latitude 40°N)

Ursa Minor
Ursa Major
Camelopardalis
Cassiopeia
Cepheus
Draco

## Winter Constellations (Evening Sky)

| Northern Sky | Southern Sky |
|---|---|
| Pegasus | Cetus |
| Lacerta | Taurus |
| Andromeda | Orion |
| Pisces | Eridanus |
| Triangulum | Lepus |
| Aries | Canis Major |
| Perseus | Monoceros |
| Auriga | Canis Minor |
| Gemini | Gemini |
| Cancer | Hydra |

## Spring Constellations (Evening Sky)

| Northern Sky | Southern Sky |
|---|---|
| Auriga | Virgo |
| Gemini | Corvus |
| Lynx | Crater |
| Canes Venatici | Leo |
| Boötes | Hydra |
| Corona Borealis | Cancer |
| | Gemini |

## Summer Constellations (Evening Sky)

| Northern Sky | Southern Sky |
|---|---|
| Coma Berenices | Equuleus |
| Canes Venatici | Delphinus |
| Boötes | Aquila |
| Corona Borealis | Scutum |
| Hercules | Ophiuchus |
| Lyra | Serpens Caput |
| Vulpecula | Virgo |
| Cygnus | Libra |
| Lacerta | Scorpius |

## Autumn Constellations (Evening Sky)

| Northern Sky | Southern Sky |
|---|---|
| Corona Borealis | Pisces |
| Hercules | Aquarius |
| Lyra | Equuleus |
| Cygnus | Capricornus |
| Lacerta | Sagittarius |
| Pegasus | Ophiuchus |
| Andromeda | Scutum |

# Life Cycles of the Stars

## Nebulae and Star Birth

In between the stars are regions of gas and dust known as *nebulae* (neb'yoo-lee; singular form: nebula, neb'yoo-le). Many of these regions are visible through binoculars, though they show only as faint hazy regions in the sky, looking almost like clouds. The colors, like those in the photograph below, are too faint for the eye to see. Only long exposures will bring out the colors. Still, it is fun to search the sky to see these hazy shapes.

There are several types of nebulae. Some, like the Horsehead Nebula shown below, contain both glowing gas and dark, light-absorbing dust. The dark dust prevents us from seeing farther. Many of the stars on the image are young stars, formed from the gas and dust in the nebula.

The Pleiades (p. 56) are a cluster of stars embedded in dust. Some of the light from the stars in the Pleiades is reflected to us by the dust. The result is a *reflection nebula.*

Glowing gas, light-absorbing dust, and reflection nebulae are kinds of *diffuse nebulae.*

The Horsehead Nebula, which is below the leftmost star in Orion's belt. Dark dust absorbs light from behind it to make the horsehead.

Another type of nebula is called a *planetary nebula*, though it has nothing to do with planets. It got its name because in telescopes, some planetary nebulae look like small greenish disks, as do the planets Uranus and Neptune. The Ring Nebula, shown below, is one of the easiest to see with a small telescope. It then looks like a faint hazy smoke ring; only a long photographic exposure reveals its colors.

Planetary nebulae form when stars like the sun reach the end of their normal lifetime of 10 billion years or so. The sun is about halfway through its lifetime, so we think it will become a planetary nebula in about 5 billion years. First the sun will swell to become a huge, cool star known as a red giant. Then the outer layers of the red giant will drift off into space and become a ring or shell. The hot, lower layers of the star will then become visible as the bluish central star of the planetary nebula.

Stars more massive than the sun will come to a different end: they will explode as supernovae. The remnants left behind may spread into space and become diffuse nebulae. The Crab Nebula in Taurus and the Veil Nebula in Cygnus are examples of exploded stars of this type.

The Ring Nebula in Lyra, a planetary nebula. Note its hot, bluish central star. The gas in the nebula was thrown off this star during the last 50,000 years.

# Stars and Clusters

The stars are all balls of gas held together by their own gravity. Our sun is an average star. It is about 15,000° C (27,000° F) at its center and about 6,000° C (11,000° F) at its surface. One million Earths could fit inside it. Some stars are about 15 times less massive than the sun, while others are 60 times more massive. Stars can be about 3 times cooler than the sun and about 10 times hotter.

When you heat an iron poker in a fire, first it glows dimly red, and then brighter red hot. If it could be made still hotter, it would become blue-white. Similarly, the coolest stars are the reddest ones. Moderately hot stars, like the sun, are yellowish in color. The hottest stars are blue-white. In the constellation Orion, for example, Betelgeuse (in the shoulder) is a cool, reddish star. Rigel (in the heel) and the stars in the belt are blue-white, hot stars (see p. 11). Astronomers describe the temperatures of stars' surfaces with a series of letters: O B A F G K M, where O stars are the hottest and M stars are the coolest. The sun is a G star.

Though the sun is a single star, most stars have close companions. These *double stars* have two or more stars orbiting around each other, bound together by their mutual gravity. In most cases, it takes years or centuries for the stars to complete one orbit around each other.

The Beehive Cluster, an open cluster of stars in Cancer. The planet Jupiter is the bright overexposed object at left.

Many stars appear in star clusters, which come in two basic types. *Open clusters* contain hundreds of stars, and have no particular shape. We merely see stars especially close together in the sky. These stars have all formed out of the same interstellar gas and dust. The stars are still young, perhaps "only" hundreds of thousands or millions of years old. The Pleiades in Taurus (p. 56), the Hyades in Taurus, and the Beehive Cluster in Cancer are open clusters that are easy to see with the naked eye or binoculars.

*Globular clusters* are groups of hundreds of thousands of stars held together in a compact ball. The stars orbit the center of the cluster. They are all very old, about 10 billion years in age. M13, the thirteenth object on Messier's list (see p. 60), in Hercules is the easiest globular cluster to see in the northern sky. The bigger the telescope you use, the better you can see the individual stars in a globular cluster.

Omega Centauri, a globular cluster in Centaurus.

# White Dwarfs and Supernovae

When a star—a hot ball of gas—uses up the nuclear fuel near its center, it collapses. How it ends up depends on how much mass it had. A star with as much mass or less mass than the sun gives off a planetary nebula. The nebula's central star cools to become a white dwarf, a tiny star containing perhaps as much mass as the sun but compressed into a size no larger than the Earth. Each teaspoonful of a white dwarf contains many tons of matter. No white dwarfs can be seen with the naked eye. The easiest to detect is Sirius B, a companion to Sirius, though it takes a medium-sized telescope to do so.

When a white dwarf is in a double-star system, it can gain some mass from its companion. When a little mass hits the white dwarf and undergoes fusion, the star brightens. We see such a brightening as a *nova*. A nova is visible to the naked eye every few years. Sometimes the white dwarf gains so much mass that it collapses again. It is incinerated, and the star brightens tremendously. Such an event is one kind of *supernova*.

The other kind of supernova occurs when a star more massive than the sun transforms all the hydrogen in its core to iron. Then the star collapses, and completely explodes (see facing page).

Supernovae of either kind are very rare. A few are detected by astronomers each year, but almost always in distant galaxies. No supernova has been seen in our own Milky Way galaxy since the year 1604, five years before the telescope was invented! Nobody saw the supernova of 1667, whose radio image we now detect (see p. 48). The first time a supernova was seen with the naked eye since 1604 was in 1987. This supernova, shown in the photographs opposite, became brighter than 3rd magnitude. It occurred in the Large Magellanic Cloud (p. 81), a companion galaxy to our own, and was visible only from more southern latitudes than our own.

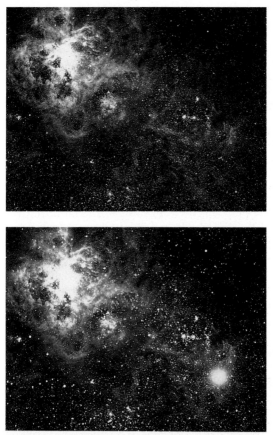

The supernova *(bottom)* was seen in the Large Magellanic Cloud in 1987 as a bright star appearing where only a supergiant star had been barely visible *(top)*.

# Pulsars and Black Holes

A supernova blasts its outer layers into space. Sometimes we can see the remnant centuries later. The Crab Nebula, below, is the remnant of a supernova that went off over 900 years ago. Though it was the first object Messier listed in his catalogue, it is not especially interesting to look at with a small telescope.

The gas in the midst of many supernovae is pressed together during the explosion. It collapses until it becomes a tiny *neutron star*, with as much mass or slightly more mass than the sun. All this mass is contained in a space only about 10 kilometers across, the size of a city. We usually cannot see neutron stars directly, for they are so small and faint. But we can detect some of them from the radio waves they send out. Some send out beams of radio waves that sweep around the sky as the neutron stars rotate, just as a beam of light from a lighthouse sweeps around the sky. We detect a pulse of radio waves every time one of these beams passes the Earth, and we call the objects *pulsars*. The pulsars we know of can rotate as often as 642 times each second or as slowly as once every 4 seconds, still very rapid for a full-fledged star.

A handful of pulsars, including the one in the middle of the Crab Nebula, can be detected optically, but only with large telescopes. The pulsar in the Crab Nebula flashes 30 times each second.

The Crab Nebula, M1, the remnant of a supernova explosion seen on Earth in 1054.

Sometimes the core of a supernova has too much mass to stop collapsing at the neutron-star stage. The dying star's gravity, pulling itself inward, is too strong. The star keeps collapsing forever. When such a star gets smaller than a certain size, it warps the space around it so much that not even its light gets away to reach us. We can think of it as having gravity strong enough to pull back its light. We call these objects *black holes.*

Black holes don't give off light so we cannot see them directly. We can, however, detect x-rays from the gas just outside the black holes. This gas is in orbit around the black holes. Satellites orbiting above our atmosphere, which keeps the x-rays from reaching the Earth's surface, have revealed to us a handful of such probable black holes. The best-known case is in the constellation Cygnus.

To decide that a black hole is present, astronomers look at the double-star systems from which flickering x-rays are received. By studying whether the single star they see is moving to and fro, they can tell if it has an invisible companion. The hot gas orbiting a black hole may look like the bright gas in the painting below.

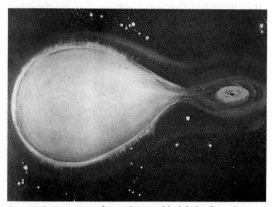

An artist's conception of gas orbiting a black hole after it leaves the companion star.

# Galaxies

Our sun and all the stars that we can see are members of a much larger group, called the Milky Way Galaxy, which contains about a trillion stars plus much gas and dust in between the stars. Most of the stars of the Milky Way Galaxy are in a giant disk 100,000 light-years across—the distance that light travels in 100,000 years.

The Milky Way that we see stretching across the nighttime sky is the plane of the disk of the Milky Way Galaxy. From our position two-thirds of the way out, we cannot see through the disk all the way to the center of our galaxy because there is too much gas and dust. However, when we look toward the center of our galaxy we see somewhat more stars, gas, and dust. This difference explains why the Milky Way looks brightest in the constellation Sagittarius, the direction of the center of our galaxy. In that direction, we see the part of the Milky Way Galaxy that is richest in star clusters and nebulae.

Some galaxies are elliptical in shape; our own is a spiral. Here we see the giant elliptical galaxy M87 in Virgo. It is unusual in that it has a jet of gas that shows the presence of violent action in its center.

Many galaxies, like the one shown below, look like our own. It is called the Whirlpool Galaxy, and can be seen in small telescopes a few degrees south of the star at the end of the handle of the Big Dipper. It is 15 million light-years away, relatively close for a galaxy. That is, the light we are seeing now from that galaxy took about 15 million years to reach us, even at the tremendously high speed at which light travels (300,000 kilometers per second = 186,000 miles per second).

The Whirlpool Galaxy, the Great Galaxy in Andromeda (p. 50), and our own Milky Way Galaxy are all *spiral galaxies*, with arms unwinding in spiral form. The Great Galaxy in Andromeda is the closest spiral to our own and thus the easiest to see.

Near the Great Galaxy in Andromeda are two smaller galaxies. These smaller galaxies are *elliptical galaxies*. Though these elliptical galaxies are relatively small, other elliptical galaxies can be quite large. With a medium-sized telescope, you can see many galaxies of all kinds.

The Whirlpool Galaxy (M51) in Canes Venatici, with another small galaxy at the end of one of its spiral arms. Our own Milky Way Galaxy is also a spiral, though its arms are not quite as open as in this galaxy.

Galaxies are so far away that we can never travel far enough in the universe to see them from another view. To learn about galaxies, therefore, we must look at many of them. We see some of them, like the one below, from the side (edge on); others are tilted at an angle so we can see more of their arms. Note how the dark dust lane in the photo below is narrowly limited to the plane of the galaxy.

Galaxies are the basic building blocks of the universe. Astronomers are now mapping how the galaxies are distributed in space. Our galaxy, the Great Galaxy in Andromeda, and about two dozen other galaxies make up the Local Group of galaxies, which in turn is part of a cluster of many galaxies. Clusters of galaxies (see p. 83) seem to be linked in giant filaments that stretch across the universe. In among the filaments are giant voids where few or no galaxies are found.

It is fun to locate a few galaxies with binoculars. With small telescopes, you can find a larger variety of galaxies, though it is a challenging task.

This galaxy, known as the Sombrero Galaxy, is seen edge on.

If you ever travel far enough south, toward the Earth's equator or into the southern hemisphere, the pair of galaxies shown below makes a pretty sight to the naked eye or to binoculars. These galaxies are called the Large Magellanic Cloud and the Small Magellanic Cloud, since Magellan's crew saw them when they sailed around the world in the 16th century. You must be near or below the equator for them to appear high in the sky.

The name "Cloud" is apt, for at first each of these galaxies resembles a hazy white cloud in the sky. They also look like a bit of the Milky Way that has become detached.

The Magellanic Clouds can be seen only from more southerly latitudes. Here the Large Magellanic Cloud is near the top and the Small Magellanic Cloud is near the bottom.

# The Past and Future of the Universe

Astronomers can measure how fast objects in space are moving toward or away from us, and they have discovered that all the distant galaxies are moving away from our own. The farther away a galaxy is, the faster it is moving from us. In other words, the universe is expanding. Our view is like that of someone on a raisin in raisin bread dough that is rising. No matter which raisin you stand upon, all the other raisins are moving away from you. The farther one is away, the faster it is moving away, since there is more material expanding between you and it.

There is, however, no center to the expansion of the universe. The universe fills all space, and space expands as the universe expands. The study of the universe and its past and future is called *cosmology.* Cosmology is advanced by theoretical studies and by studies made with many telescopes on the ground and in space.

Astronomers know the universe is expanding, and we can all see what it was like in the past. Studies tracing the galaxies back in time show that about 12 billion to 20 billion years ago, all the matter would have been compressed together. Astronomers have concluded that the universe's expansion began with a Big Bang, which also marked the origin of time.

Astronomers have even detected signals in space that started traveling across space soon after the Big Bang. With the passage of billions of years, the signals have changed so that they are now received as radio waves. The discovery of these radio waves from the early period of the universe is a proof that the universe did begin in a Big Bang.

What will the universe do in the future? Will it expand forever? Will it ever contract? Astronomers study this problem, but do not know the definite answer. Nonetheless, we can tell, from our universe's current rate of expansion, that it would not begin contracting for at least 50 billion years.

A current theory of cosmology holds that during the first second of time the universe became rapidly bigger, that is, it inflated. Now, the theory goes, the universe's rate of expansion is slower. The inflationary-universe theory concludes that the universe will keep expanding forever but at a slower and slower rate. Eventually it will be just at the dividing line between expanding and contracting.

Studies made on the ground and from space, and with telescopes studying not only light but also radio waves, infrared light, ultraviolet light, x-rays, and gamma rays from space, may one day give us a better idea of our future.

A cluster of galaxies, a location in space where many galaxies are close together.

# Planets and the Solar System

Our sun is surrounded by many smaller objects. Nine of these objects are known as planets. Mercury, Venus, Mars, Jupiter, and Saturn were known even to the ancients. Uranus was discovered in 1781, Neptune in 1850, and Pluto in 1933. Planets orbit the sun in elliptical paths. The farther out the orbit, the longer a planet takes to complete it.

From night to night, the planets mostly drift westward in the sky with respect to the stars. Occasionally, a planet reverses the direction of its drift for some weeks. This effect occurs as the Earth passes nearest to the other planet, just as a car may appear to move backward as you pass it.

In addition to the major planets, minor planets, also called *asteroids,* orbit the sun. The largest is about 1000 kilometers across. Most of the 3000 asteroids now known have orbits between the orbits of Mars and Jupiter. Others, however, come inside the Earth's orbit. Every few hundred thousand years, an asteroid of moderate size may hit the Earth and do a lot of damage.

The sun is also surrounded by a giant cloud of many objects made of ices—frozen gases—of various materials such as water and methane. Some of these objects are nudged out of their distant orbits in the cloud, far beyond Pluto, and fall into the inner solar system. When these objects get close enough to the sun, the gas and dust in them are pushed out into a tail by the sun's light and by its expanding gas. We see the objects as comets (see p. 100).

Scientists have studied almost all the planets and a couple of comets from spacecraft. The views from spacecraft have revealed aspects of the planets, their surfaces, and their atmospheres that we could not find out from Earth-based telescopes. In the pages that follow, we discuss each of the major objects of the solar system in turn, and give some hints on observing them.

# Solar System Data

| Planet | Radius of Planet (km) | Radius of Orbit (million km) | ÷ Earth's | Time for Orbit (yr) |
|---|---|---|---|---|
| Mercury | 2.439 | 58 | 0.4 | 0.24 |
| Venus | 6.052 | 108 | 0.7 | 0.62 |
| Earth | 6.378 | 150 | 1.0 | 1 |
| Mars | 3.393 | 228 | 1.5 | 1.9 |
| Jupiter | 71.400 | 778 | 5.2 | 11 |
| Saturn | 60.000 | 1.427 | 9.5 | 29 |
| Uranus | 26.200 | 2.871 | 19.2 | 84 |
| Neptune | 24.300 | 4.497 | 30.1 | 165 |
| Pluto | 1.160 | 5.914 | 39.5 | 249 |

| Moons | Radius of Moon (km) | Radius of Orbit (km) |
|---|---|---|
| Mercury: none | | |
| Venus: none | | |
| Earth: | | |
| the Moon | 1738 | 384.500 |
| Mars: | | |
| Phobos | 13 × 10 × 9 | 9.378 |
| Deimos | 8 × 6 × 5 | 23.459 |
| Jupiter: | | |
| Io | 1815 | 422.000 |
| Europa | 1559 | 671.000 |
| Ganymede | 2631 | 1.070.000 |
| Callisto | 2400 | 1.885.000 |
| plus over a dozen smaller moons | | |
| Saturn: | | |
| Mimas | 195 | 185.600 |
| Enceladus | 255 | 238.100 |
| Tethys | 525 | 294.700 |
| Dione | 560 | 377.500 |
| Rhea | 765 | 527.200 |
| Titan | 2575 | 1.221.600 |
| Iapetus | 730 | 3.560.000 |
| plus over a dozen smaller moons | | |
| Uranus: | | |
| Miranda | 242 | 129.800 |
| Ariel | 580 | 191.200 |
| Umbriel | 595 | 266.000 |
| Titania | 805 | 435.800 |
| Oberon | 775 | 582.600 |
| plus at least 10 smaller moons | | |
| Neptune: | | |
| Triton | 1300 | 354.000 |
| Nereid | 170 | 5.570.000 |
| plus smaller moons | | |
| Pluto: | | |
| Charon | 600 | 19.000 |

## MERCURY

Mercury, the planet closest to the sun, has a very hot surface. As it rotates slowly under the sun, its surface temperature reaches 400°C (800°F). It is so close to the sun in the sky that it is visible only in the west for the hour or so after sunset or in the east for the hour or so before sunrise. At the times it is visible, it appears as a bright, steadily shining object. Many people have never seen Mercury. Often it is too close to the sun to be seen at all.

Our view of Mercury from Earth must always pass through the turbulent air near the horizon. Our best views of Mercury were from the Mariner 10 spacecraft in 1974 (see photo below). Like our own moon, Mercury is an airless body covered with craters. Mercury also shows some lines of cliffs, as though the planet shrank when it cooled soon after its formation.

Mercury, as photographed from the Mariner 10 spacecraft.

# VENUS

Venus is about the same size as Earth. However, it is closer to the sun and as a result has become much hotter. Its thick atmosphere traps solar energy inside, making the temperature at Venus' surface 500°C (900°F)—hot enough to melt even lead. The heat is trapped by the *greenhouse effect:* sunlight comes through Venus' clouds and heats Venus' surface, which gives off infrared rays, but the water vapor and carbon dioxide in the atmosphere do not allow the infrared rays to pass through.

Venus can be the brightest object in the sky other than the sun and moon. It can gleam brilliantly in the western sky for two hours or more after sunset or in the eastern sky for two hours or more before sunrise. It is thus often called "the evening star" or "the morning star." Often Venus shines steadily, but if the air is very turbulent it can appear to change color to red and green. A telescope reveals that Venus goes through a set of phases, from crescent-shaped to mostly full.

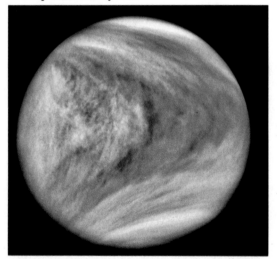

NASA's Pioneer Venus spacecraft sent back this picture of the tops of the clouds around Venus. Only about 2% of the sunlight hitting the tops of the clouds filters down to the planet's surface.

s been visited by many spacecraft. United States and the Soviet Union. Radar, which bounces radio waves off an object, penetrates the clouds and has been used to map Venus' surface. Scientists using a small radar on a spacecraft near Venus have found that Venus is mostly covered with a vast rolling plain, and has continents. Venus also has volcanoes, which may well be active. The largest is more than 1500 kilometers across. This volcano, and some other parts of Venus, can also be mapped with powerful radars on Earth.

Spacecraft that have landed on Venus have survived for only a few hours because of the high temperatures and pressures. The spacecraft have sent back photographs of flat rocks like rocks found on Earth, and of an orange sky.

Studying Venus' atmosphere helps us understand our Earth's. We already have a greenhouse effect of our own and must be careful not to add enough carbon dioxide or other gases to our own atmosphere to make it heat up as Venus' has.

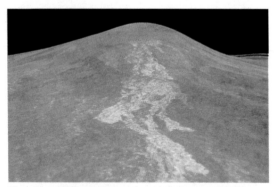

The volcano Sif Mons on Venus, shown in a computer projection (with the height magnified 10 times) based on radar data from NASA's Magellan spacecraft.

## EARTH

The Earth, our own planet, is an oasis in space. The view from space has shown it to be a haven from the harsh conditions that exist at most other places in the solar system.

We now know that the Earth is very active geologically. The continents rest on large flat *plates* that drift slowly around the Earth's surface. Two hundred million years ago, the continents separated from one original land mass or continent. Understanding continental drift, by studying the Earth and comparing it with other planets, can help us understand and predict earthquakes and volcanoes.

Tides in the Earth's oceans are mostly caused by the moon. The moon's gravity pulls water on the near side of the Earth toward the moon, and pulls the solid body of the Earth away from water on the Earth's far side. Thus, in most places on Earth, we have two high tides every day.

Astronauts en route to the moon took this picture of Earth, showing oceans, the North American continent, and clouds.

## MARS

Mars appears reddish in our sky, even to the naked eye. Since its orbit around the sun lies outside the Earth's orbit, Mars can be opposite the sun in the sky. Thus it can be up in the sky at any time of the night. About every two years, Mars and Earth are in the parts of their orbits that are closest together. At those times, Mars appears relatively bright—brighter than the brightest star—and, to a telescope, relatively large. At other times, it can be as faint as 2nd magnitude and relatively small.

In the martian springtime (which occurs separately in each hemisphere, as on Earth), the surface of the planet changes color. Long ago, it was thought that vegetation might be turning color, indicating that life existed on Mars. We now know that the color change is caused by seasonal winds on Mars covering and uncovering darker surfaces with reddish dust. The Viking spacecraft that landed on Mars in 1976 found no signs of life.

In binoculars, Mars looks like a small reddish disk. Even moderate-sized telescopes do not show its surface features well.

Mars, photographed with the Hubble Space Telescope. The Syrtis Major region appears prominently.

In 1976, when the twin Viking spacecraft traveled to Mars, one part of each spacecraft went into orbit around Mars and the other part landed on the surface of Mars. The orbiters found giant volcanoes, larger than volcanoes on Earth. They also found vast cratered regions and a canyon as long as the United States measures from coast to coast.

The landers photographed boulders of a wide range of sizes. The sky on Mars appears pink because of the pinkish dust suspended in it. The Viking spacecraft worked for many years, and sent back information about the winds and weather on Mars and how they change with the seasons. The martian atmosphere is very thin; at the surface the atmospheric pressure is only 1% of the Earth's atmospheric pressure.

Mars has two small moons, Phobos (from the Greek word for "fear") and Deimos (from the Greek word for "terror"), named after the mythological companions to the war god, who was called Mars in Rome. These moons are always fainter than 11th magnitude, and cannot be seen from Earth except with large telescopes.

The surface of Mars in the vicinity of the Viking 2 lander. Note the boulders and the pinkish sky.

## JUPITER

Jupiter is the largest of the planets. It is mostly a ball of gas, 11 times larger in diameter than the Earth. Its rocky core contains more mass than the Earth does.

Jupiter can be very bright in the nighttime sky, brighter than the brightest star. Since its orbit around the sun is outside that of the Earth, it can be on the opposite side of the Earth from the sun. Thus Jupiter may well be seen at midnight or at any other hour during the night.

Through binoculars, one can easily see Jupiter's four largest moons: Io, Europa, Ganymede, and Callisto. They were discovered by Galileo in 1609, using one of the first telescopes. Today's binoculars are more powerful than Galileo's telescopes. If you watch Jupiter's moons for an hour or more, you can see they are moving with respect to Jupiter; within hours you can tell that they are orbiting Jupiter.

Even a small telescope shows two or more dark bands on Jupiter. The steadier the air in our atmosphere, the more bands you see.

Jupiter, photographed with the Hubble Space Telescope. The Great Red Spot, a giant storm, is at lower right.

The Voyager 1 and 2 spacecraft visited Jupiter, and sent back images from close up (see below). Jupiter's Great Red Spot, larger than Earth, is a circulating storm that has been present for hundreds of years. The Voyagers also sent back close-ups of Jupiter's moons which revealed that many of them are worlds unto themselves. They have mountains, craters, valleys, and, in the case of Io, many erupting volcanoes.

This montage made from Voyager images shows Jupiter, with its Great Red Spot, and several of its larger moons. Callisto is at lower right, Europa is visible in front of part of Jupiter, Ganymede is at lower left, and reddish Io is at left.

## SATURN

Saturn is usually the prettiest object to be seen in the sky, since even a small telescope shows the beauty of its rings. They are chunks of ices and rock orbiting Saturn. Though now we know that Jupiter, Uranus, and Neptune also have rings, only Saturn's are spectacular when seen at a great distance.

Saturn shines as a steady, yellowish light in the nighttime sky, and can be up at any hour. A small telescope used in steady air will show not only the rings but also a dark gap in the rings, called the Cassini division. The limit in our ability to see detail is usually caused by the unsteadiness in the Earth's atmosphere rather than by a lack of magnifying power; giving a telescope more magnifying power usually only enlarges the blurry image but does not make it clearer.

Saturn's moon Titan is one of the largest moons in the solar system. From Earth, it can be seen with binoculars or a small telescope as a point of light near Saturn.

The Voyager spacecraft visited Saturn and its moons, and sent back close-up images, including the one below. Since Saturn is farther from the sun and therefore colder, the chemical reactions that create colors work more slowly in its clouds. As a result, we see fewer contrasting bands on

Saturn, photographed with the Hubble Space Telescope.

Saturn's surface than on Jupiter's. The Voyagers discovered that Saturn's rings were really made up of many thousands of thin ringlets.

The spacecraft photographed several of Saturn's moons and discovered new ones. Titan has an atmosphere that is even thicker than Earth's, and the surface pressure on Titan is higher than Earth's. Its reddish color comes from a type of smog. Other satellites of Saturn bear cracks, ridges, craters, and many other types of features. Mimas bears a crater so large that the moon must have nearly broken apart during the crater's formation.

A montage from Voyager 1 images of Saturn and its larger moons. Clockwise from top left we see Titan, Mimas, Tethys, Dione, Enceladus, and Rhea, reproduced at far from their relative sizes to give the effect of perspective.

## URANUS

Uranus, discovered in 1781, was the first planet that had not been known to the ancients. It is so far away that we knew little about it until Voyager 2 flew close by in 1986. Until then, Uranus and its moons had been little more than points of light in even a large telescope. In 1977, when Uranus passed in front of a star, the star's light winked off and on a few times before and after the planet itself hid the star. From this information, astronomers discovered that Uranus was surrounded by nine narrow rings.

The Voyager 2 spacecraft imaged the rings, but did not provide much more information than astronomers had from their ground-based studies. Voyager 2 did, however, send back the high-resolution image of Uranus' surface shown below. Uranus is so far from the sun that its surface is almost featureless. It looks blue-green because methane gas in its clouds absorbs all the other colors. A few individual clouds were barely visible in high-resolution images. By tracing the motion of these clouds, astronomers learned that Uranus rotates on its axis every 17 hours.

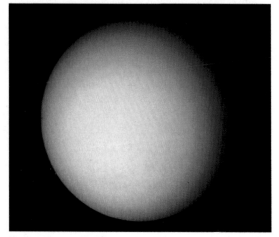

Uranus, photographed from Voyager 2.

The moons of Uranus, on the whole, are darker than most of the moons of Saturn, which are icy. Voyager 2 was affected by the gravity of the most massive moons as it passed them, and could measure how much mass they had. From this information and the moons' sizes, scientists deduced that Uranus' moons are mixtures of rock and ices of water, ammonia, methane, and other chemicals.

The five largest moons of Uranus, those known before the spacecraft visited, are named after characters in Shakespeare's *A Midsummer Night's Dream* and *The Tempest* and in Pope's *The Rape of the Lock*. All Uranus' moons have craters on them. Ariel shows faults on its surface, a sign that geological activity has taken place. Umbriel, about the same size, is completely and uniformly covered with craters. Titania shows few large craters, indicating that material flowed out from its surface to cover them. Oberon has many large craters. Miranda, though smaller, has so many different kinds of features on its surface that it obviously underwent some kind of geological activity.

Miranda. Though this moon is small, with a radius of only 242 kilometers (150 miles), it shows a banded region and a region including ridges, valleys, and impact craters. We see geologic faults and lines of cliffs, and signs that material has erupted.

## NEPTUNE

Neptune, about the same size as Uranus and four times larger in diameter than Earth, remains almost unknown to us. It was discovered in 1846, as the result of mathematical predictions based on its gravitational effect on Uranus. Like Uranus, Neptune is mostly gas surrounding a liquid ocean and a rocky core.

Neptune has two moons. Triton, named after a sea god in Greek mythology who was one of Poseidon's sons, is larger than our own moon. Nereid, from the Greek word for "sea nymph," is much smaller and farther away from Neptune.

Neptune has passed in front of a few stars recently, and by studying the way the stars' images were blocked, astronomers have found that the planet also has some material in rings.

The Voyager 2 spacecraft reached the Neptune system on August 24, 1989. Neptune has several giant storms, the largest of which is the Great Dark Spot. Neptune's rings encircle the planet but are clumpy. Triton's icy surface has quite varied terrain and several ice volcanoes. Six additional moons were discovered.

Neptune, photographed from Voyager 2, showing the Great Dark Spot.

## PLUTO

Pluto, the planet with the largest known orbit around the sun, was discovered in 1933. It is about 14th magnitude, so you would need a moderate-sized telescope to see it.

In 1978, an astronomer realized that Pluto's image in a large telescope was not quite round, and that the bulge shown in the image below was a moon. The presence of the moon, named Charon, has allowed astronomers to measure Pluto's mass. Pluto turns out to be much less massive than had been thought—only about 1/500 the mass of the Earth.

Pluto and Charon have been passing in front of each other as they orbit each other. By studying the light as it is blocked, astronomers now have determined accurate sizes for both objects. Pluto is only two-thirds the size of our moon, and Charon is half of Pluto's size. Pluto and Charon are certainly very different from the giant planets Jupiter, Saturn, Uranus, and Neptune. Perhaps the two were once moons of Neptune.

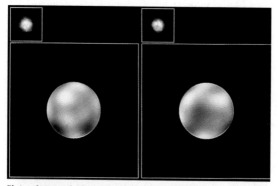

Pluto, photographed with the Hubble Space Telescope.

## Comets

Comets can be especially beautiful to see, but only rarely do bright ones appear in our sky. Whenever you hear from the newspaper, radio, or television that a bright comet will be in view, be sure to see it. You may get only a few days' notice.

Comets are chunks of ice that have been long orbiting the sun far beyond Pluto's orbit. The gravity of the matter in the plane of the Milky Way Galaxy or of a passing star sometimes pulls one of these chunks of ice out of its distant orbit. It falls in toward the sun. As it nears the sun, the ice turns into gas and releases the dust in it. Both stream away from the sun in separate tails. The head of the comet contains the icy nucleus with a larger *coma* of gases around it.

Halley's Comet, which last returned in 1986, is the brightest comet that appears at regular intervals. It won't be back until 2061. Comets Hyakutake in 1996 and Hale-Bopp in 1997 appeared brighter to the eye and had longer tails. Most bright comets do not give much advance notice.

Halley's Comet as seen in 1986.

The advance notice of the return of Halley's Comet enabled many large telescopes to be trained on the comet and a flotilla of spacecraft from many nations to be sent to visit it, leading to important discoveries. We now know a lot more than we did about the gases in a comet and how they are released.

Photographs of the nucleus of Halley's Comet from the European Space Agency's Giotto spacecraft revealed that the nucleus is potato-shaped and is only 15 km × 10 km. The mission confirmed the idea that the comet is a dirty snowball. It is covered with a dark crust that reflects only about 2% of the sunlight that hits it. On the sunlit side, jets of gas and dust come out of a few cracks in the crust. The gas and dust eventually sweep around the nucleus to make the tail.

The tail of a comet can extend millions of miles into space, always in the opposite direction from the sun. It has been said that a comet's tail is the closest thing to nothing that anything can be.

Halley's Comet in 1986, with the yellowish dust tail and the bluish gas tail coming back from the head that includes the coma and nucleus.

## Meteors

As comets orbit the sun, dust spreads out in their orbits. Eventually, the comet itself becomes defunct, either because it uses up most of its ices or because its nucleus is covered with a crust. Still, the dust remains in orbit around the sun. Whenever the Earth passes through the dust, the dust burns up in the Earth's atmosphere. We see these dust grains burning up as shooting stars, called *meteors.*

The Earth travels along the same orbit through the solar system each year, so meteor showers occur yearly. The easiest shower to see is the Perseids, so called because the meteors appear to radiate from the constellation Perseus if we trace them back across the sky. We see them, however, all over the sky. The Perseids occur on August 11 or 12 each year, a conveniently warm time to view the skies outdoors.

No equipment is needed to see a meteor shower. Just lie on your back on a lawn chair or blanket, and look up. You may see a meteor every minute or so during the Perseids and Geminids. Even when a meteor shower is not taking place, you should see a random meteor in the sky approximately every 10 minutes. You will see more meteors after midnight than before, since then the Earth has turned so that we are plowing into interplanetary dust.

A wide-field time exposure several minutes long with an ordinary camera may reveal meteors.

## Meteor Showers

| Date | Name | Nights Visible |
| --- | --- | --- |
| January 3 | Quadrantids | 1 |
| April 21 | Lyrids | 2 |
| May 4 | Eta Aquarids | 3 |
| July 28 | Delta Aquarids | 7 |
| August 11 | Perseids | 5 |
| October 21 | Orionids | 2 |
| November 3 | South Taurids | weeks |
| November 17 | Leonids | weeks |
| December 13 | Geminids | 3 |
| December 22 | Ursids | 2 |

## *Asteroids*

In addition to the nine major planets, thousands of minor planets, or *asteroids*, orbit the sun. Most of them are in the asteroid belt between Mars and Jupiter. Some dozens, however, cross the Earth's orbit, and may hit the Earth from time to time.

The largest asteroid, Ceres, is more than 1000 kilometers across. Vesta, over 500 kilometers across, can become bright enough to be barely visible with the naked eye. You can see more asteroids with binoculars, if you know where to look.

When someone is taking an astronomical photograph using a camera or telescope that tracks the stars, making the stars appear as points of light, asteroids will appear as streaks, since they move at a different rate across the sky.

# The Moon

The moon is the brightest object in the sky aside from the sun. The moon can be seen whenever it is up, even in the daytime sky if it is clear enough.

The moon, which is more than one-fourth the Earth's diameter, orbits the Earth at an average distance of 384,000 kilometers (238,000 miles). With respect to the stars, the moon takes 27 days, 7 hours, and 43 minutes to complete each orbit. The Earth has moved in that time, so it takes 29⅓ days for the moon to come back to the same place in our sky.

In that 29⅓-day period, the moon goes through a whole cycle of phases. The phase we see depends on the relative positions of the Earth, the moon, and the sun. When the moon is on the far side of the Earth from the sun, we see all of the half that is sunlit. We call this phase a *full moon*. When the moon is one-fourth of the way around its orbit in the direction across the sky toward the sun, we call the phase the *third-quarter moon*. When the moon is halfway around its orbit, in more or less the same direction from us as the sun, we have a *new moon*. About a week later, when the moon is another one-fourth of the way around, we have the *first-quarter moon*.

At the first-quarter and third-quarter moons, half the disk of the moon we see is lighted. When less than half the disk is lighted, we see a *crescent moon*. When more than half is lighted, we see a *gibbous moon*.

During the approximately two weeks from new moon to full moon, we see more and more of the moon each night. The moon is *waxing* (see photos). From full moon to new moon, we see less and less of the moon each night. The moon is *waning*.

On a clear night, you can see the unlighted part of the disk of the moon, even when only a crescent is lighted. This "old moon in the new moon's arms" occurs because some light from the sun reflects off the Earth onto all of the moon's disk that is facing us.

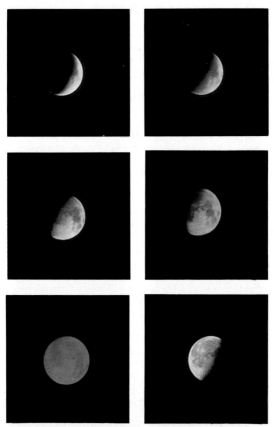

At top, two crescent phases of the moon as it waxes. Mare
Crisium is the small oval lunar sea at right. From below it,
extending diagonally upward to the left, we see Mare
Fecunditatis, Mare Tranquillitatis, and Mare Serenitatis. The
crater Tycho, which has light-colored rays of dust stemming
from it across the lunar surface, is barely visible in the first-
quarter-moon image at left in the second row. Next are a gibbous
waxing moon and a full-moon image. In the full-moon image,
Oceanus Procellarum is the mare at extreme left, with Mare
Humorum and Mare Nubium below it. Mare Imbrium is to its
upper right. Finally, we see the waning moon near third quarter.

Since the full moon is opposite the sun in the sky, it necessarily rises as the sun sets. Thus the full moon rises at sunset and is up all night. The moon rises about 50 minutes later each day. About a week later, we have a third-quarter moon, which rises at midnight. The new moon, about a week later, rises around sunrise, but we usually don't notice it since it is up in the daytime. It sets at sunset. A couple of days later, we see a crescent in the west at sunset. After a few more days have passed, the first-quarter moon rises at noon, and so is high in the sky at sunset.

Galileo, in 1609, discovered craters and flat areas called maria (mar'ee-ya; singular: mare, pronounced mar'ay, from the Latin for "seas"). You can see even with your naked eyes that parts of the moon are darker than others. Binoculars or a telescope will reveal the craters and maria.

When trying to use charts showing the moon's maria and craters, remember that though binoculars give an image oriented the same way the image appears to your eye, most telescopes give an inverted image. That problem is easy to overcome by turning your moon chart upside down. However, some telescopes have an extra mirror in the eyepiece—a "diagonal mirror"—that allows you to look into the telescope from the side. Such a mirror flips the image from side to side.

The full moon is always opposite the sun in the sky, so it rises at sunset.

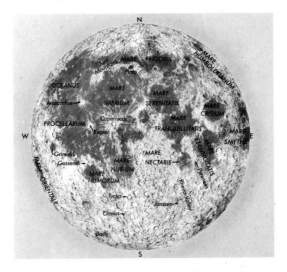

*Top:* A drawing of the moon, in a projection that spreads out the regions near the edge to make them more visible. (Courtesy of the National Geographic Society and the U.S. Geological Survey) *Bottom:* The moon's orbit around the Earth is elliptical, so at different times it appears to be different sizes in the sky. Also, we see the effect of *libration*, which enables us to see around the edge different amounts at different times.

The moon's orbit is tilted 5° with respect to the Earth's, so usually the moon does not pass exactly into the Earth's shadow each month. When it does, we have a lunar eclipse, with the sun, Earth, and moon in a line. The dark part of the Earth's shadow, the *umbra* of the shadow, takes about 2 hours to cover the moon. The total part of the lunar eclipse may last an hour or so. Some of the red part of the sunlight is bent around the Earth through the Earth's atmosphere, so the totally eclipsed moon may appear faintly red. A lunar eclipse can be seen by anyone for whom the moon is up. The total lunar eclipse of September 15–16, 1997, will be visible from the rest of the world but not in the Americas. The partial lunar eclipse of the morning of July 28, 1999, will be visible from every continent. The next total lunar eclipse visible from the Americas will occur on January 20–21, 2000.

The crescent moon seen in the western sky soon after sunset. Venus is near it. Earthshine—sunlight reflected off the Earth—allows us to see "the old moon in the new moon's arms."

The totally eclipsed moon *(top)* glows faintly reddish because of light from the sun that has passed through the Earth's atmosphere. The sequence below shows the progression of phases of a lunar eclipse over nearly 3 hours. The camera's shutter was left open much longer for the total phase.

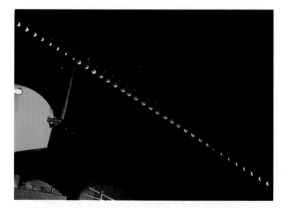

The moon was visited by a series of American unmanned and manned spacecraft, including the Apollo missions that brought 12 astronauts to the moon during 1969–72. The astronauts took many measurements on the moon, left behind reflecting mirrors to bounce back laser beams from Earth, and carried home a total of 382 kilograms (842 pounds) of moon rocks to be analyzed on Earth.

The astronauts and scientists analyzing the data discovered that the craters on the moon were formed by meteorites—rocks from outer space hitting the moon's surface. A few craters, like Copernicus and Tycho (p. 107), show rays of light-colored material thrown out in the impact. The rays darken with time, so Copernicus must be one of the younger lunar craters, perhaps only a few hundred million years old. Most of the other lunar features have been in place for billions of years. The highland rocks, the heavily cratered regions, were formed between 4.42 and 3.9 billion years ago. Lava flowed over the lunar surface to form the maria (lunar seas) between 3.8 and 3.1 billion years ago. The few craters in the maria formed after that time.

The Lunar Module of the Apollo 11 mission in 1969 climbing back toward the parent spacecraft orbiting over the moon, with the Earth in the background.

During the later Apollo missions, the astronauts got around the moon on a Lunar Rover *(top)*. The lunar crater Eratosthenes *(bottom)*, photographed from the Command Module orbiting the moon.

# The Sun

The sun is our nearest star. It differs from other astronomical objects mainly in that we can observe it only in the daytime. The sun is so bright—magnitude −27—that its light scatters around in the Earth's atmosphere to make the sky bright. The blue part of the sun's light scatters more efficiently than its red light, so the daytime sky is blue.

The sun is so bright that it can burn your retina—the back part of the inside of your eye —if you stare at it. So never stare at the sun, and never look at the sun through binoculars or telescopes unless special solar filters are in place.

You can make a solar image to see by projecting it onto a screen. You can use binoculars or a small telescope to do so, adjusting the focus so that the image is clear on the screen when you hold the binoculars or telescope about 1 meter (3 feet) from the screen. You should look *only at the image on the screen*, and never up at the sun through the binoculars or telescope.

When you look at a solar image, you usually see a few dark regions—*sunspots*—on the sun. Each sunspot is a region of the sun that is about 1000°C cooler than the rest of the surface. The sun's magnetic field is concentrated there.

The number of sunspots on the sun rises and falls with a period of about 11 years. 1994–95 was the most recent time of sunspot minimum, the part of the cycle when few sunspots were visible on the sun. In about 2000, we will have sunspot maximum, when there will be many spots on the sun every day. Then the number of sunspots will wane again.

If you become more interested in solar observing, you can purchase special filters that will show more structure on the sun's surface or above the sun's edge, as below. The number of features that can be seen also varies with the sunspot cycle.

The kinds of features we see on the sun presumably also exist on other stars, though the other stars are too far away to see in such detail.

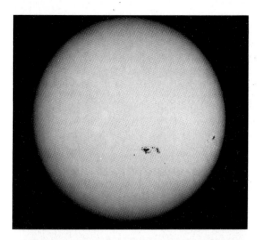

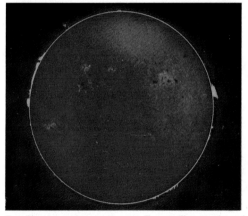

*Top:* The sun, with sunspots on it. *Bottom:* The sun, through a special solar filter that passes only the light emitted by hydrogen gas. Solar prominences are seen off the sun's edge on a longer exposure; the superimposed shorter exposure shows dark sunspots as well as other solar phenomena.

Because of the tilt of the moon's orbit with respect to the Earth's, the moon does not pass exactly between the Earth and sun each month. But about every year and a half, the moon does pass exactly between the Earth and sun and blocks the sunlight from reaching a small region of Earth. As the sun, moon, and Earth move in space, the shadow cast by the moon sweeps a long, thin path across the Earth. Along this path—thousands of kilometers long and as much as hundreds of kilometers wide—we see a *total solar eclipse.*

A total solar eclipse is the most spectacular astronomical sight that exists. Over a period of an hour or two, the moon gradually blocks the sun. The darkening of the sky is noticeable only during the last few minutes of this time. Finally the sky grows rapidly darker, as less and less sun is visible. Then the moon covers the entire bright disk of the sun. As it does so, the sun shines through a few valleys on the edge of the moon. These bright beads of light are Baily's beads. The last Baily's bead glows so brightly that it looks like a diamond on a ring, creating the *diamond-ring effect* (see p. 116). Then the total part of the eclipse—*totality*—lasts for a period of time that could be as short as a few seconds or as long as 7 minutes. At the end of totality, we briefly see the diamond-ring effect again, and then the total phase is over. The bright solar surface comes out from behind the moon, and the sky brightens.

During totality, the sky around the sun is dark enough that we can see stars, even though it is daytime. Near the horizon, however, we can see far enough to get light from regions where the eclipse is not total. Because, as at sunset, we are looking through a lot of air, we see a reddish horizon all around, like a 360° sunset.

Eclipses look so beautiful because of a lucky circumstance—the moon is 400 times closer than the sun and also 400 times smaller. Thus the sun and the moon take up almost exactly the same angle in the sky, and the moon can block the sun exactly.

114

Though an eclipse occurs somewhere on Earth every year and a half, it takes more than 300 years on the average for an eclipse to pass your particular location. So people travel to see the beauty of solar eclipses. The February 26, 1998, total solar eclipse will cross Panama, Columbia, Venezuela, and the Caribbean islands Aruba, Curacao, Guadeloupe, Antigua, and Montserrat. The August 11, 1999, will cross from England's Cornwall, northern France, Germany, Switzerland, Austria, Hungary, Romania, Turkey, Iraq, Iran, Pakistan, and India. The total eclipse of January 21, 2001, will cross southern Africa.

Sometimes, the moon is relatively far from the Earth in its elliptical orbit and does not quite cover the sun during an eclipse even when it passes centrally across it. An annulus — a ring — of sun remains visible. Annular eclipses will be visible from Indonesia and Malaysia on August 22, 1998, and from Australia on February 16, 1999.

The solar corona—a halo of hot gas at a temperature of 2,000,000°C—surrounds the dark disk of the moon in the sky in this view during a total solar eclipse.

115

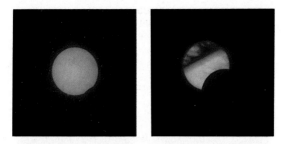

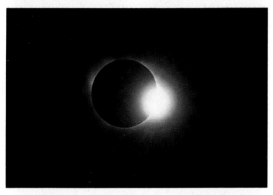

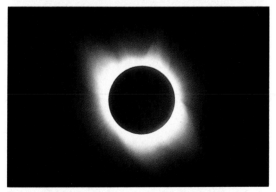

Phases of a total eclipse. At top are partial phases, one with a cloud silhouetted. Then the diamond ring (p. 114) follows. The bottom image shows the solar corona, a halo of 2,000,000°C gas surrounding the everyday surface of the sun.

116

## Observing Eclipses

The sun is so very bright that it can harm your eyes if you stare at it for more than several seconds or if you look at it directly through binoculars or a telescope. During the total part of an eclipse, the part of the sun you see—the solar corona—is only as bright as the full moon, and so is not hazardous to look at. In an annular eclipse, the solar surface is never fully covered, so do *not* look at it directly.

*To view the partial or annular phases of an eclipse, it is best to make a pinhole camera.* Simply make a hole a few millimeters across in a piece of opaque cardboard. Hold this cardboard up to the sun, and you can make an image of the partially eclipsed sun fall onto a second piece of cardboard. Look only at this second piece of cardboard, not up through the hole. Alternatively, you may purchase a solar filter or make your own by holding unrolled black-and-white film (not color film) out in the sunlight for a few seconds (to expose it uniformly) and then developing it. One or two layers of the developed black-and-white film will make a good solar filter.

If you are lucky to be in one of the few spots on Earth where the sun is totally eclipsed, make sure you look directly at the sun during the total phase; do not miss the spectacular show. Then turn away when the sun's bright everyday surface comes out again.

*Left:* Standing under a tree during the partial or annular phases of an eclipse makes pinhole images of the sun fall on you; the "pinholes" are the spaces between the leaves. *Right:* You can safely look at the partial or annular phases of an eclipse through a special solar filter.

117

# Tips on Observing

## Observing with Your Naked Eye

The first and best way to start observing the stars and other bodies in the universe is with your eyes. Even without the aid of a telescope or binoculars, your eyes make fine detectors for light from the stars.

When you are in a bright room, however, the cells in your retina become bleached and your eyes are not very sensitive. When you go out into the night, your pupils widen right away. They can become 8 millimeters across, instead of the 2 or 3 millimeters across they were inside. But your retina stays bleached for a while. It may take as long as 15 minutes for your eyes to become *dark adapted.* You will find yourself seeing more and more stars as this time passes.

Be careful during this time not to look at any white lights. Red light will not interfere with your adaptation to darkness, so you can use a red flashlight (or put red cellophane over an ordinary flashlight).

With your naked eyes, you can see the sun, the moon, and stars as faint as 6th magnitude. In particular, you can see all the stars on the star maps in this book. You can see traces of one or two globular clusters, such as M13 in Hercules (p. 60), and the galaxy M31 in Andromeda (p. 50).

You can see five planets with the naked eye: Mercury, Venus, Mars, Jupiter, and Saturn.

You can study certain stars with your naked eye, comparing them with other stars to notice variations in brightness. Every 3 days, Algol drops a factor of 3 in brightness over the span of an hour; Betelgeuse changes in brightness over months. You can see Alcor and Mizar as a double star.

If you are lucky, you can see a comet. Comets may stay visible to the naked eye for a few days or a few weeks.

All in all, naked-eye astronomy can be a lot of fun.

## Observing with Binoculars

Binoculars gather light and funnel it to your eyes. Thus you can see fainter things with binoculars than you can with your naked eye. You can also see more detail.

Binoculars are rated by two numbers: the magnifying power and the diameter of the front lenses. For example, 7 × 50 binoculars magnify 7 times and collect light with a pair of lenses, each 50 millimeters across. Since your eye opens to 8 millimeters across at best, a binocular lens collects a lot more light than your eye.

For astronomy, you are more concerned with collecting light than with magnification. 7 × 50 is the most popular size binocular to use for astronomy. Binoculars with higher magnification cannot be handheld without shaking too much; you could use them on a tripod or other base.

With binoculars, you can see not only the stars on the maps but can also tell that many of them are double. You can see many nebulae, such as the Orion Nebula, and can see star clusters much better. You can see 10 or more stars in the open cluster known as the Pleiades instead of the six to eight most people see with the naked eye. If you sweep along the Milky Way, you will find many clusters and nebulae on your own.

Prisms or mirrors inside binoculars reflect the light entering the lenses. Use binoculars without your eyeglasses (if you wear them), and adjust the focus with the central knob to compensate for your nearsightedness or farsightedness. Binoculars usually also have an adjustment on one of the eyepieces to allow for a difference between eyes.

## Observing with Telescopes

Telescopes collect light and funnel it to your eye or to a photographic plate or television detector. They are thus types of "light buckets." The magnification effect of telescopes is less important.

Some telescopes collect light using a front lens. These are *refracting telescopes*. Popular refracting telescopes often have lenses 5–10 cm (2–4 inches) across. Some telescopes collect light using a rear mirror. These are *reflecting telescopes*. Popular reflecting telescopes often have mirrors 10–20 cm (4–8 inches) across. The image quality of a refracting telescope, noticeable when observing the planets, is often equivalent to that of a reflecting telescope about twice as large.

Compound telescopes that are now very popular have a mirror in the rear but also have a thin lens at the front. The lens allows telescope makers to use a spherical mirror, which is easier to make and allows a wider field of view, rather than a more complicated paraboloidal mirror that can be used without a front lens. The compound telescopes are usually of the Schmidt-Cassegrain design, in which the light that passes through the front lens is reflected up by the spherical main mirror and is then reflected down by a secondary mirror through a hole in the main mirror, where it is conveniently accessible for an eyepiece or camera.

A Newtonian telescope is a type of reflector in which the light is reflected up the tube by the main mirror, and then out to the side with a flat mirror.

The most important thing to look for when you are buying a small telescope is, surprisingly, the quality of the mount. Many people buy a small telescope and then find that the mount is too unsteady to hold an object in view or to find an object easily. Sturdy mounts are not cheap, but it is a waste of money to buy a telescope with a flimsy mount.

Once you have a telescope, you can collect a lot of light, which will allow you to see much fainter objects. Also, you can see finer detail, such as the rings of Saturn. You will see more star clusters, and more individual stars in them. You will see more types of nebulae and more structure in them. You will see many more galaxies.

Your telescope will probably be on a mount that tracks the stars as they move across the sky. Since the stars appear to move around the Earth once each 24 hours, a simple 24-hour motor attached to a properly aligned—*equatorial*—mount allows the telescope to keep up with the stars. If you have this kind of mount, you can place a camera back (without the lens, because the telescope acts as the lens) on the telescope, and take pictures of clusters, galaxies, and nebulae. Or you can attach a camera with its lens on top of the telescope, taking a long exposure while the telescope tracks.

Even without a telescope, you can use fast color films to take constellation photos. Just put your camera on a sturdy tripod, and try exposures 2, 4, 8, 16, 32, and 64 seconds long.

Happy cbserving.

This 20-cm (8-inch) Schmidt-Cassegrain telescope passes starlight through a thin lens, reflects it with a main mirror up to a small mirror on the back of the front lens, and then passes it through a hole in the main mirror to the eyepiece.

# Time

Time on our watches is based on the motion of the sun. Basically, when the sun passes due south, it is noon. However, that system would mean that any person on a different line of longitude would have a different solar time. In 1884, a series of *time zones* was set up; each person in a certain time zone has the same time. Time jumps, usually by a whole hour, at the edge of a time zone.

When it is six o'clock at night in the summer, it is still light out. To give us more time to spend outdoors in daylight, most states (though not Arizona, Hawaii, or parts of Indiana), have adopted *Daylight Saving Time,* setting the clock forward by one hour in the spring (the first Sunday in April) so that 6 P.M. becomes 7 P.M. In the fall (the last Sunday in October) we set our clocks back by one hour. Remember, "Spring forward, Fall back."

Astronomers often keep time by the sun's position in relation to the zero line of longitude, the meridian of Greenwich, England. They use this *Universal Time* (U.T.) so data from all over the world can be easily compared. Astronomers use sidereal time to remember when certain stars are up, since a given star or constellation rises at the same sidereal time each day.

Time measured by the stars, *sidereal time* (p. 68), matches solar time at the fall equinox, around September 21. Then sidereal time grows earlier than solar time by 3 minutes 56 seconds each day. At the spring equinox, sidereal time is 12 hours earlier than solar time.

## Time Zones

| From U.T. to | Standard Time | Daylight Time |
|---|---|---|
| Atlantic Time | −4 hours | −3 hours |
| Eastern Time | −5 hours | −4 hours |
| Central Time | −6 hours | −5 hours |
| Mountain Time | −7 hours | −6 hours |
| Pacific Time | −8 hours | −7 hours |
| Alaska Time | −10 hours | −9 hours |
| Hawaii Time | −10 hours | |

# Calendars

Every time the Earth goes around the sun, a year passes. This process takes about 365.25 days. Thus, after a year, the Earth has turned an extra ¼ turn than a mere 365 rotations. After four years, the Earth has completed one whole extra rotation—an extra day. We thus add an extra day to our calendars every fourth year, making it a leap year. Ordinarily, years that are divisible by four—1988, 1992, 1996—are leap years.

The system was set up by Julius Caesar, who named July after himself. Augustus Caesar named August after himself, and took a day from February to make August as long as July. At that time, the year began in March, which explains why September, October, November, and December come from the roots of the Latin words for 7, 8, 9, and 10.

A year is actually slightly shorter than 365.25 days: it is 365.2422 days long. To keep from getting ahead of ourselves, we now omit the leap year every hundredth year. Thus 1700, 1800, and 1900 were not leap years. However, every 400th year, we do have the leap year after all, so the year 2000 will be a leap year.

A year is defined from the interval between passages of the sun by the *vernal (spring) equinox,* one of the two points at which the ecliptic (see p. 17) and the celestial equator (see p. 6) cross. The *autumnal (fall) equinox* is the other crossing. The word "equinox" means equal night, but the lengths of day and night are not actually equal at the spring and fall equinoxes. For one thing, the Earth's atmosphere bends light from the sun, making it appear to rise when it is really still a few degrees below the horizon. Also, the equal lengths of day and night would apply to time when the center of the sun rises, but daylight starts when the top of the sun rises. Thus the daytime is about 10 minutes longer than the nighttime at the equinoxes, and equal day and night precede the vernal equinox and follow the autumnal equinox by a few days.

## Acknowledgments

I thank Naomi Pasachoff, Elizabeth Stell, Marian Warren, Anne T. Pasachoff, Eloise Pasachoff, Deborah Pasachoff, and Eric Kutner for reading a draft, and Harry Foster and Barbara Stratton for their editing. Wim van Dijk assisted Wil Tirion with airbrush work on the sky backgrounds and the Milky Way in Wil's beautiful star maps.

Star maps by Wil Tirion
Constellation paintings by Robin Brickman

### Picture Credits

# *Index*

Page numbers in *italic* refer to illustrations.